OPERA GUIDE 26

Rosina Storchio, the creator of the title role, La Scala, 1904 (Stuart-Liff Collection)

26

Madam Butterfly
Madama Butterfly

Giacomo Puccini

Opera Guide Series Editor: Nicholas John

John Calder · London
Riverrun Press · New York

Published in association with English National Opera

COPYRIGHT DATA

First published in Great Britain, 1984, by John Calder (Publishers) Ltd, 9-15 Neal Street, London WC2H 9TU

First published in the U.S.A., 1984, by Riverrun Press Inc., 1170 Broadway, New York, NY 10001

Second Impression 1990

BRITISH LIBRARY CATALOGUING IN PUBLICATION DATA

Puccini, Giacomo
Madam Butterfly.— (Opera guide; 26)
1. Puccini, Giacomo. Madama Butterfly
2. Operas—Librettos
I. Title II. Illica, Luigi III. Giacosa, Giuseppe
IV. John, Nicholas V. Series
782.1′092′4 ML410.P89

LIBRARY OF CONGRESS CATALOGING IN PUBLICATION DATA
Puccini, Giacomo, 1858-1924.
[Madam Butterfly. Libretto. English & Italian]
Madame Butterfly.

(Opera guide; 26)
Opera libretto, in Italian with English translation, by Luigi Illica and Giuseppe Giacosa, based on David Belasco's play Madame Butterfly.
Bibliography: p. 128
Discography: p. 126
Includes Index.
1. Operas—Librettos. I. Illica, Luigi, 1857-1919. II. Giacosa, Giuseppe, 1847-1906.
III. Belasco, David, 1853-1931. Madame Butterfly. IV. Title. V. Series.
ML50.P965B62 1984 84-755703

ISBN 0-7145-4038-2

English National Opera receives financial assistance from the Arts Council of Great Britain.

Typeset in Plantin by Maggie Spooner Typesetting, London NW5.

Printed in Great Britain by The Southampton Book Company, Southampton.

CONTENTS

Page

LIST OF ILLUSTRATIONS

Images of the Orient

Jean-Pierre Lehmann

'Globe-trotting' is an expression dating from the Victorian period when gentlemen (and a few ladies) of leisure chose to embark on adventurous escapades across the world. Improvements in transport on land and sea — the establishment of the Orient Express, the opening of the Suez Canal — offered greater and more rapid opportunities for travel, while the suppression of piracy and the widespread military, diplomatic and commercial representation throughout the world of the major Western powers reduced the risk of making overseas travel more exciting than had been bargained for. On the whole, by the last quarter of the nineteenth century the chances of completing one's travel in the cauldron of some hostile tribe, or similar misfortunes, were remote.

While the merchants, sailors, diplomats, missionaries and assorted travellers who ventured to distant lands may have represented a very small proportion of the European population, they were avid communicators. Keeping a journal was far more often done then it is now and publishing accounts of one's adventures fairly common. Although these writers may have described realities — as they saw them — they also significantly contributed to the creation of images and hence nurtured dreams of exotic lands among their compatriots. Furthermore, the use of these settings for novels, poetry, plays and operettas increased an appetite for imaginary travels to foreign countries.

Partly because it was one of the last countries to be 'opened' to the West, partly because it was the furthest away in the Far East and partly because of the tales which travellers unravelled on their return, Japan became a 'must' for the Western traveller. While today Pierre Loti's *Madame Chrysanthème* (1887) and Giacomo Puccini's *Madam Butterfly* (1904) are the best known works of fiction with a Japanese setting, there was, in fact, a vast quantity of lesser known but quite popular works of the same genre. Also, in the late nineteenth and early twentieth century there occurred in the artistic and cultured circles of Europe the fashion known as *japonisme*: the impressionist painters, Whistler, the Goncourt brothers and their circle, and later, William Butler Yeats and Ezra Pound, to name but a few, drew inspiration from Japanese art and perceptions of Japanese culture.

The great designer *par excellence* of the Western image of Japan was a half-Greek half-Irish journalist-adventurer by the name of Lafcadio Hearn. Hearn had been brought up in Ireland in considerable hardship and in 1869, at the age of nineteen, he left for the United States. Then followed twenty years of a difficult, frequently impoverished, career as a journalist. He arrived in Japan in 1890, initially on a two-year assignment. In fact he became infatuated with the country, and this inspired his literary talents. He lived in Japan until his death in 1905, married a Japanese and eventually became a Japanese citizen, changing his name to Koizumi Yakumo. Hearn had been both unhappy and generally unsuccessful in the West. His exhilarated espousal of Japan, therefore, was in great part motivated by his bitterness against the West and everything the West stood for: no doubt reflecting his Irish upbringing, his most vitriolic scorn tended to be reserved for Roman Catholicism.

In his fifteen years in Japan, Hearn, apart from teaching English, wrote with prolific zeal. Along with countless articles for newspapers and journals, he produced on average one book *per annum*. With titles such as *Glimpses of Unfamiliar Japan* (1894), *Out of the East* (1895), *Kokoro* (which means 'heart' in Japanese), *Gleanings in Buddha-Fields* (1897), *Exotics and Retrospectives* (1898), *Japan: a Miscellany* (1901), and perhaps his masterpiece, *Japan: an Attempt at an Interpretation* (1904), many of which were translated into several European languages, Hearn captivated the European imagination. His conversion from the West to an unconditional faith in the moral and aesthetic superiority of Japanese civilisation was not totally exceptional among Western writers and artists. Another example was the American professor of art and philosophy, Ernest Fenollosa, who was invited to Japan in the 1880s to teach Western art, but quickly became an *afficionado* of Japanese art and subsequently sought to infuse the United States with the spirit of Far Eastern civilisation.

The Western image of Japan can be said to have consisted of two major elements. On the one hand, Japan was perceived as a society which had achieved a very high degree of aesthetic accomplishment. Japanese art was highly appreciated for its simplicity and purity, and so the Japanese were extolled for their spiritual values at a time when European artists saw their own society as excessively materialistic. In the salons of the upper bourgeoisie a *japoniste* flavour of interior decoration became fashionable: an illustration can be seen in Manet's portrait of Emile Zola surrounded by Japanese wood-block prints. Japanese-style gardens also came into vogue.

Another striking image, and one which was complementary to that of the artistic universe, was of a country inhabited by graceful, charming — and complaisant — women. Exoticism inevitably conjures up images of sensuality. Projected onto Japan, these images were fortified by descriptions of certain Japanese customs, notably mixed-bathing and, of course, of the institution of geisha-houses. The *veni-vidi-vici* theme of 'Western boy meets Japanese girl' was taken up by many writers of the day — and, over the decades, it became the most popular one.

To what extent did the image of Japan merge with reality? Japanese art was highly developed and sophisticated. Compared to most countries which Western travellers would visit, Japan was relatively free of extreme poverty; it was certainly not dirty: traditional Japanese architecture and the general aspect of the towns were undoubtedly pleasing to the eye. The Westerner would also reside in Japan in far greater security than was the case elsewhere. Whereas for rather more than a decade, following the 'opening' of the country in 1854, xenophobic samurai sought to expel Westerners forcibly by means of terrorism — in a movement known as *joi*, 'expel the barbarians' — by 1868 the official policy of the government was not only to acquiesce in the opening of the country, but indeed to learn from the West. Nothing comparable to the Indian Mutiny of 1857 or the Chinese Boxer Uprising of 1900 came to mar relations between Europeans and Japanese. On the contrary, once the Japanese had become avid pupils of Western civilisation, they tended to treat Westerners themselves with admiring curiosity, courtesy and respect.

What Japan desired to learn from the West, however, was how to become a major industrial and strong military power. The government-inspired slogan of the period, *fukoku kyohei* ('rich country and strong army'), encapsulated the objectives to which the nation as a whole should

Emmy Destinn, the first exponent of the title role at Covent Garden, in 1905 (Royal Opera House Archives)

aspire. Hence the 'aesthetic universe' was being modernised with telegraph poles, railway lines, industrial factories. Office buildings were built along Western lines, with bricks and mortar, and furnished with wooden chairs and tables. The process of 'Westernisation' included a major sartorial revolution, in which men (usually, but also some women) abandoned traditional *kimono* in favour of Western clothes. The Japanese word for a man's suit to this day remains *sebiro*, which is etymologically derived from the place where Japanese officials in Europe began having their suits made, namely Savile Row.

Western reactions to these changes and aspirations must be considered with three major points in mind. Firstly, given the general Western outlook at a time when Europe was at the zenith of its power and superiority, that an insignificant and distant Asian nation should seek to emulate the West in terms of industrial and technological development could only be considered absurd. Secondly, however, travellers are always keen to find what they are looking for. The European travelling to Japan was primarily motivated to capture the mysteries of a distant, exotic, oriental — with all that the term 'oriental' implied — civilisation, and in the hope that enjoying the enchantment of some 'Madam Butterfly' would provide the much-anticipated extra bonus. To travel thousands of miles to Japan to discover that Osaka was no different from Manchester could hardly justify the cost and the expectations, let alone provide good material for gratifying the excited curiosity of family and friends left behind. The third point is that contact between Western visitors and residents with the Japanese was, in fact, rather limited. They tended to remain in the so-called 'treaty ports', usually Yokohama, Nagasaki or Kobe, living in the 'international settlements', areas reserved for foreign residence and commerce. The Japanese Westerners came across were mainly in subservient positions, such as employees, shop-keepers, servants and prostitutes.

The attitudes of Westerners, therefore, tended either towards simply ignoring what was going on in the 'modern' side of Japanese national life, or to dismiss it with feelings ranging from sympathy to scorn. In the 'sympathetic' category one finds, for example, Rudyard Kipling, who visited Japan in 1890 and recorded his impressions in articles which were incorporated in his two volume *From Sea to Sea* (London, 1900). Japan's attempt at 'modernisation', Kipling felt, was above all very bad taste: Japan, he urged, should stay as it is. 'The whole empire [should be put] in a glass case amd marked *Hors Concours*, Exhibit A.' He objected to the fact that 'many American missionaries in Japan . . . instil into the Japanese mind wicked ideas of 'progress' and teach that it is well to go ahead of your neighbour, to improve your situation, and generally to thresh yourself to pieces in the battle of existence.'

While Japan may have been admired for its art, therefore, and travellers to the country envied for the enchanting 'mousmes' — as Japanese girls were then generally called in Western literature, taken from the Japanese *musume*, meaning daughter or young girl — they would encounter, as a modern, industrial nation with military strength it was not taken very seriously. The image of a hedonistic, somewhat ridiculous country, was vividly reproduced in Pierre Loti's *Madame Chrysanthème* (1887). This set a fashion for stories with Japanese settings: Puccini's opera was actually based on a play which the American playwright, David Belasco, had adapted from a magazine story by John Luther Long (1898). Despite minor characters and situations borrowed from Loti the opera is significantly different in approach.

Loti had, of course, been to Japan whereas Long, Belasco and the

Mario Sammarco as Sharpless and Giovanni Zenatello as Pinkerton, the roles which they created at La Scala, 1904 (Stuart-Liff Collection)

collaborators on the opera had not. In this novel, Loti, a naval officer, expresses the two objectives he has for his stay in Japan: one is to be tattooed, the second is to acquire a temporary Japanese wife, namely for the duration of his visit. The first objective is achieved at the end of his stay and the result is much to his satisfaction. Not so when he sets about getting his 'wife'. The service Loti was looking for was very common in Japanese treaty ports at the time. It was a question of perusing the girls that were on offer, making a choice and negotiating a price. This was, therefore, a straight commercial transaction, containing absolutely no romantic flavour. Having acquired his wife 'O-kiku-san', that is Miss Chrysanthemum, in fact Loti finds her fickle and tiresome. He does admit once to a slight twinge of jealousy as he notices that there seems to be a hint of mutual infatuation between O-kiku and his friend Yves, but by and large he longs to be rid of her. His antipathy for O-kiku is generously extended to all her compatriots, as he develops an intense dislike of the Japanese, whom he consistently refers to as monkeys. Finally, when his ship is due to sail, he takes leave of O-kiku, who makes all the appropriate sighs and wailings of farewell. Having forgotten

Salomea Kruscenìski as Cio-Cio-San, the first to sing the role in the revised version of May, 1904 in Brescia. This Russian soprano included Brünnhilde, Isolde, Tatyana, and Salome in her repertory, and was the first to sing Elektra in Italy. 'Recordings reveal a voice of great beauty, spanning a range of two and half octaves.' HR (Stuart-Liff Collection)

something in his room, he returns after this touching scene, to see O-kiku happily counting her money and waiting for her next 'husband'. There is little here in common with the sentiments evoked by Butterfly, nor is there anything very beautiful or tragic about what actually boils down to a rather sordid episode.

Loti's story is undoubtedly more realistic than the opera. While there were romantic encounters and marriages between Westerners and Japanese girls 'de bonne famille', the Loti-O-kiku-san type arrangement was far more prevalent. The girls thus employed in the treaty ports tended to be from rural communities, whose parents hired or sold them off to city traders in order to help make ends meet. They were only in the business for the money. It is equally clear that, although Messager's operatic version of *Madame Chrysanthème* (1893) continued to be successful in the first decades of this century, there was not going to be much mileage for Puccini in its ironic tone and unsentimental character while he was immediately attracted by the atmosphere of Belasco's play (which he saw at the Duke of York's Theatre in 1900 while visiting London for the Covent Garden première of *Tosca*). He must also have found an affinity in the deep and complex character of Butterfly. She belongs with the nun in *Suor Angelica* or Liù in *Turandot* to the number of his heroines who die for love. Hence while the setting is Japan, with the exotic images it still produced, and Pinkerton like Loti is a sailor, and O-kiku and Cho-cho practice the same profession, the resemblance ends there. Compared to the rather coarse Chrysanthème, Butterfly has a far more beautiful character, and her story is far more touching.

Loti's disparaging view of Japan confirmed the assumptions of Europeans who refused to recognise the major industrial and military changes taking place in the country. The consequences, as indicated by the scholar William Schwartz (in *The Imaginative Interpretation of the Far East in Modern French Literature*, Edinburgh and Paris, 1926), could be rather unfortunate:

The importance of Loti's writings on Japan lies in their reiteration in

> exquisite language that the Japanese is a monkey, endowed with a grotesque and perverted refinement of taste, but without morals. He suggests that the Japanese women, the 'mousmes', have no honour, and that the race can have nothing in common intellectually with Europeans. I believe that the contempt for the Japanese expressed in Loti's books in some measure influenced the Russians to refuse Japan's requests and led to the war of 1904. The Russian Court was open to French influence, and many Russian naval officers of high rank, following Loti's example, had discovered *Madame Chrysanthème*. Like Loti, the Russian Court looked upon Japan with contempt, and chose to believe his stories because Loti shared their prejudices.

It is in fact ironical that the first performance of *Madam Butterfly* at La Scala, on February 17, 1904, occurred exactly nine days after the opening salvoes of the Russo-Japanese war. A year later Japan won a military victory over Russia which astounded — and indeed alarmed — the West. Between the images conjured up in *Madam Butterfly* and the realities of the naval battles of the Tsushima straits — where the Japanese under Admiral Togo annihilated the Russian fleet — there is an awesome gap.

The image was not, however, totally eradicated. Until the 1930s, when, for obvious reasons, the *Madam Butterfly* image of Japan disappeared, the theme survived and manifested itself in various literary guises, notably in the novels of John Paris and in the interwar Western 'classic' on Japan, Thomas Raucat's *L'Honorable Partie de Campagne* (translated into English as *The Honourable Picnic*). Thomas Raucat is in fact a *nom-de-plume* of a Frenchman by the name of Poidsatz, who chose Thomas Raucat because it is a homonym of the Japanese word *tomaro-ka*, which can be translated as 'shall we spend the night here'. After the war the image reappeared in novels

Geraldine Farrar as Cio-Cio-San, one of her most famous roles, at the Met. in 1907 (Stuart-Liff Collection)

such as Richard Mason's *The Wind Cannot Read* and James Michener's *Sayonara*, as well as in many films (often starring William Holden).

The city of Nagasaki, the setting for *Madam Butterfly*, was brutally destroyed by the second atomic bomb dropped on Japan in August 1945. Sometime thereafter, and for rather obscure reasons, a statue of 'Madam Butterfly' was erected. It can be found on the estate turned monument of one of Nagasaki's first and foremost Western residents, an Aberdonian by the name of Thomas Glover, a successful merchant in the mid-nineteenth century and, among other things, responsible for first introducing Scotch whisky to Japan. The statue is based on fiction and perhaps, more than that, reflects a history of relations between Japan and the West of cultural misunderstanding, of chasms between Western images of Japan and Japanese reality.

While in one sense *Madam Butterfly* may have, as a theme, epitomised Western insensitivity and illusions regarding Japan, there is, however, another more positive side to the encounter between the two cultures. It was indicated above that the Japanese had become avid students of the West. They certainly achieved significant strides in becoming a modern industrial and military power; since 1945 their industrial and technological developments have left their former mentors in many cases well behind. The Japanese also, however, absorbed a great deal of Western culture and nowhere, perhaps, is this more visible than in music. Not only are they now very receptive to Western music, but they have become major performers. It is in that sense, therefore, that while the historical origins of *Madam Butterfly* may represent a not particularly harmonious period in the meeting of two cultures, its main significance today is simply the quality of its art. Herein lies its universal appeal and hence the fact that Japanese opera-goers and performers are, like everyone else, indebted to Loti and O-kiku-san who, however indirectly, gave birth to *Madam Butterfly*.

Lisa della Casa as Cio-Cio-San (Stuart-Liff Collection)

Tribulations of a Score

Julian Smith

At the première of *Madama Butterfly*, February 17 1904, Puccini and all those taking part in the new opera had the highest hopes of success. As it turned out, the performance was a disaster. Opera audiences in Italy often make their feelings known audibly while the performance continues, but the noisy reaction to the new score at times made it impossible to hear either singers or orchestra. Puccini and his cast had to endure boos and cat-calls, shouts and laughter.

Some composers would have found it difficult to recover from such a blow. Puccini, however, had what was for him an unusual degree of confidence in *Butterfly*. Encouraged by the support of friends, and especially of his publisher, Giulio Ricordi, he set about repairing the damage caused by the opening night.

Some cuts and revisions were made, the long second act was divided into two, and an aria was added. In the new form, the opera was given at Brescia just over three months later on May 28. Both composer and publisher were extremely apprehensive, and nothing was spared to ensure the work's success.

Ricordi himself was unable to be at the performance, but instructed his son Tito, the producer, to telephone him after each act with news of the audience's reaction. The performance was a great success and Puccini and Ricordi were delighted. It might be assumed that after the Brescia performances the way was clear for *Butterfly* to be presented in opera houses all over the world. This was not to be the case. Puccini took considerable trouble over the next two and a half years to ensure that a failure of the kind that had occurred at Milan could never be repeated. To this end, he arranged with Ricordi that no performance could be given without the cast and conductor first being approved by the composer. The demands of the title-role, and indeed of Pinkerton, are great, and Puccini's standards were very high. Consequently performances of *Butterfly* were few and far between, since the composer would entrust the opera only to singers and conductors whom he felt would guarantee its success. Ricordi grew quite anxious at one point that Puccini was being too fussy, and warned him that if he was always to insist on singers such as Caruso, then the opera would finish up on the bookshelves. Gradually however the work was introduced to other Italian opera houses, and to London, New York and cities as far removed as Budapest and Alexandria. On most of these occasions Puccini himself travelled to supervise the final rehearsals, and Tito Ricordi went too to oversee the production.

By June 1906, Ricordi had decided that the time had come to print a full orchestral score of *Butterfly*. Up to this time conductors had had to work from copyists' manuscript scores. The decision to print a full score suggests that both Puccini and Ricordi felt that the opera would not undergo further radical changes. The composer was pressed by Ricordi to prepare a copy of the score for the engraver. After a period of delay not uncharacteristic of Puccini, the first act was sent off to Ricordi, and its receipt was acknowledged on June 30. But at this moment, Tito Ricordi, Giulio's son, was in Paris and met Albert Carré to discuss aspects of the forthcoming

Giovanni Zenatello and Rina Giachetti as Pinkerton and Cio-Cio-San at Covent Garden, 1905 (Royal Opera House Archives)

John McCormack as Pinkerton (Stuart-Liff Collection)

French première of the opera. The director and impresario told Tito that cuts and alterations would have to be made. Carré felt that *Butterfly*, in the form it then took, would not suit the taste of Parisian audiences. His request for changes did not please Giulio Ricordi. But the engraving of the full score, about to begin, was postponed.

A series of letters and telegrams records the events of early July which had a marked effect on the score of *Butterfly*. Puccini was told on July 2 by Giulio Ricordi that Carré wished to have some changes made. Ricordi stated his own view that to agree to them would create a dangerous precedent, since then every director would impose his own ideas. He urged Puccini to consider seriously his dignity as the composer. Giulio telegraphed to Tito in Paris expressing similar views. 'We are already at the fifth version of *Butterfly*', he said, 'and we'll soon be at the twentieth if we follow the whims of directors.' Giulio was concerned about the effect a half-hearted success would have on the opera's prospects elsewhere, and he thought further changes would jeopardise the opera's chances of success in America. Tito

Joseph Hislop, who first sang as Pinkerton at Covent Garden in 1920. (Stuart-Liff Collection)

Toti Dal Monte: one of Toscanini's favourite interpreters of Butterfly, she recorded it in 1939.

Ricordi does not seem to have been in full agreement with Giulio, and urged Puccini to go to Paris to thrash the matter out with Carré. Puccini was reluctant to go, saying that while he would permit some cuts, he would not allow other alterations to the score. Eventually however he was persuaded to make the journey, Giulio having told him that Tito had provided 'convincing explanations' for the proposed changes. Puccini arrived in Paris on July 11, and in the space of a single day, to Giulio's surprise, accepted what Carré proposed, expressing himself pleased with what he was told of the planned designs and production.

With one minor exception, the Paris production of 1906, first presented in December of that year, established the familiar score of *Butterfly*.

Until recently no-one has suggested that the alterations made to *Butterfly* between the first performance and the establishment of the usual version were other than improvements. Most commentators have expressed the view that Puccini made four miscalculations in the original version which were corrected by 1907. First, there was too much realistic detail in the first act scenes with Butterfly's friends and relations, which held up the action. Second, the original Act Two, which ran continuously until the end of the opera, with the curtain remaining up throughout, was too long, and demanded too much of audiences of the time. Third, the treatment of Pinkerton in the last act disappointed the expectations of the audience, for the tenor was not given an aria, and his exit was mishandled. Finally the scene involving Kate Pinkerton was grossly insensitive and tasteless.

But these commentators have failed to acknowledge that Puccini's opera changed character significantly between 1904 and 1907. Its unconventional structure was replaced by the more usual framework of Italian opera of the period.The uncompromising, harsh, moral view of the original version was diluted until a soft-grained, sentimental atmosphere pervaded the opera.

The literary sources of *Butterfly*, John Luther Long's short novel, and David Belasco's play, as well as Illica's draft libretto of Act One, are a guide to the characters Puccini and his librettists set out to create.

Central to the changes made between the first and the traditional versions of *Butterfly* was the alteration to the character of Lieutenant Pinkerton. As depicted by John Luther Long and David Belasco he was, in Mosco Carner's words, 'positively offensive in his arrogance'. He emerges in Long's story as selfish, hard-headed, and at times cruel. 'There's no danger of you losing your head for anyone', a friend remarks to him early on. Pinkerton deliberately avoids telling Butterfly that he can give up the lease on the house at a month's notice, and leaves her with the idea that the rent will continue for nine hundred and ninety-nine years. He finds Butterfly's relations 'an appalling horde', and insults one by likening him, in his presence, to a lacquered tragedy mask. Against Butterfly's wishes he bans her relations from the house, and then encourages her to adopt Christianity, which ensures that her relations ostracise her. Later in the story the consul reflects that it was entirely like Pinkerton to take the 'dainty, vivid, eager, formless material, and mould it to his most wantonly whimsical wish', and having left her, 'he had probably not thought of her again, except as the prompt wife of another man'. In later reprints of the story Long mentioned in his preface that he had received savage letters from American sailors objecting to his portrayal of the naval officer.

In Belasco's play similar characterisation is well to the fore. We hear at second-hand from Butterfly and Sharpless of Pinkerton's slang and cruel jokes (the promise to return when the robins nest). When he eventually appears he confides to the consul that when he left Butterfly he assumed he'd no sooner be out of sight than the geisha would dry her tears and turn to testing the quality of the gold pieces he'd left her. 'You know this class of Japanese girl', he continues scornfully. Having promised his new American wife that he would speak to Butterfly about the child, the lieutenant nevertheless retreats at the sound of Butterfly's voice. He presses some dollars into Sharpless's hand, and departs, declaring weakly 'I can't face it! I'm going. Give her the money.' When he returns at the end of the play as Butterfly kills herself, it is only reluctantly, and at the urging of Kate, herself determined to gain possession of the child.

This does not altogether suggest the conventional heroic role that Italian operatic tenors are expected, and expect, to fill, yet it is clear that Illica and Giacosa, the librettists, in no way set out to modify Long and Belasco's unattractive prototype. Indeed, the first act of the opera, the librettists' own creation, actually emphasised the less appealing side of Pinkerton's

Gabrielle Lejeune as Suzuki, the first to sing the role at Covent Garden, in 1905 (Royal Opera House Archives)

character, depicting him as coarse, rude and patronising. In Illica's draft for Act One, after Goro has introduced Suzuki and the two other servants, using their long poetic names, Pinkerton declares:

> Such lovely words are wasted on such ugly things.
> Oh, here respect for customs would be a joke!
> As for me, those three monstrous things I'll call
> 'Mugs'.

And sure enough he does so in front of the assembled guests. Later, when Butterfly and her friends have arrived, Pinkerton comically mocks their high-pitched exclamations, then threatens in an aside to get his mother-in-law tight, and goes on to describe the Japanese delicacies that are served to the guests as 'sugared flies, spiders, stewed birds' nests!'.

In modifying Pinkerton's character, it was his Act Two exit which was the first element to be changed. To replace the original music Puccini constructed the arietta 'Addio, fiorito asil' ('Farewell beloved home'), — cleverly employing material from the Intermezzo to disguise the fact that the arietta was a later addition. The new scene, considered by Puccini necessary to fill a structural gap, was a mistake. It certainly made the role of Pinkerton more appealing to tenors, and it satisfied the traditional expectations of an audience for a further set-number for the leading male character. But for Pinkerton to dwell at greater length on his remorse and the realisation of what he had brought about was an error. The set-piece trio which precedes the arietta had already provided the musical and dramatic climax required to

Licia Albanese as Cio-Cio-San at the Met., where she made her debut in 1940. (Stuart-Liff Collection)

mark Pinkerton's return to the house and his meeting with Suzuki. The tension created by the prospect of his encountering Butterfly was reduced by the interpolation of the sentimental arietta, and the development of the plot was halted once again. Furthermore, a vital element in developing the full depth of the unfolding tragedy, namely that Pinkerton rushed off unable to summon enough courage to remain, was removed, since in the new version it was Sharpless who urged Pinkerton to go.

Finally, the music of 'Addio, fiorito asil' was cast in a quasi-heroic mould — an unconvincing style for the sentiments being expressed by Pinkerton.

No other alterations which affected the character of Pinkerton were made to the score until 1906. The insulting remarks passed about the servants, and the description of Japanese food remained in the score until then. So did an extra section in the Act One love duet, in which Butterfly describes how she at first visualised Pinkerton as a barbarian, but fell in love with him at first sight — a passage that was important for helping to explain her feelings for him, as well as stressing the clash of Eastern and Western cultures which lies at the root of the original story. So as the opera began to establish itself in Italy and elsewhere from 1904 until 1906, the character of Pinkerton was, with the exception of the effect of 'Addio, fiorito asil', as originally conceived. But after that time, once the insulting and patronising lines had been removed, the way was open for Pinkerton to be presented as a much more winning character, a less unworthy representative of the U.S. Navy, and a more conventional operatic tenor.

Kate Pinkerton was also given a remarkable 'face-lift' in the period between the first performance and the establishment of the normal version of the opera. Again, she was at first fashioned by the librettists on the models of Long and Belasco.

Florence Easton as Cio-Cio-San. This English soprano sang regularly at the Met. from 1917-1929. (Royal Opera House Archives)

In Long's story, Kate, who is here called Adelaide, arrives at the consulate to send a telegram to her husband, who is away from Nagasaki. She is unaware that Butterfly is in the same room, hidden by a screen hastily placed by the consul. 'Just saw the baby and his nurse' she dictates to the consul. 'Can't we have him at once? He is lovely. Shall see the mother tomorrow. Was not at home when I was there today.' She then comes face to face with Butterfly, but does not know her. 'How very charming — how *lovely* — you are dear!' she exclaims. 'Will you kiss me, you pretty — plaything.' As we shall see, Belasco preserves this last word in his play. Like her husband, Kate thinks of Japanese girls as toys, not people.

In Belasco's play Kate's aloof, condescending nature is allied to a gross insensitivity to Butterfly's situation. Arriving at the house she immediately demands to know whether Lieutenant Pinkerton, her husband, has been there. Then, confronted by Butterfly, she delivers herself of the immensely patronising line: 'Why, you poor little thing — who in the world could blame you or — call you irresponsible — you pretty little *plaything*.' She goes on to ask for the child. 'For her own good — let me take her home to my country . . . It's hard, very hard, I know', she continues, 'but would it not be better.' This scene from the play is virtually unchanged in the first version of the opera. 'I am the innocent cause of your misfortune' says Kate, and then, after asking for the child, goes on to beg Butterfly's forgiveness in a line marked *insinuante*, a description which was subsequently removed from the score when other sections of Kate's part were altered, but which is a clue to the nature of the character as at first created in the opera.

The characters of Butterfly and Sharpless were not changed by any alterations made to the score by Puccini, though there was what one might call a knock-on effect as a result of the changes effected in the Pinkertons' characters. Sharpless appears weaker in the first version. His few words of

Eva Turner as Cio-Cio-San with the Carl Rosa Opera Company in 1920 (Royal Opera House Archives)

warning to Pinkerton are clearly inadequate, and unlikely to have any effect. In the last scenes he is a mere by-stander, and fails miserably in his embarrassing attempt to persuade Butterfly to accept Pinkerton's money. Butterfly's virtues, her courage, strength and faithfulness, are of course heightened in the early version, because the contrast with the three Americans is more marked. Her dignity and restraint are immense, and were themselves emphasised by Puccini when he rewrote her final arietta for the Brescia performances. The first version of this passage projected a more resigned mood, mainly by its falling vocal line. Though marked *con esaltazione*, it was only from the second performance that it took on the truly exalted mood which provides such a climax at this point in the score.

The final set of alterations to the score requested by Carré were made when Puccini returned to Torre del Lago. The work involved the writing of a few bars here and there to cover joins, but Puccini also took out of the score all sections which included any insulting remarks made to the Japanese in the first act, as well as some illustrative detail which had previously given the wedding scene life and colour. Meanwhile Carré was working in Paris with Paul Ferrier on various alterations to the libretto. One section he changed was where Butterfly speaks of how much Pinkerton had paid for her — one hundred yen — and vows to live economically in order to spare Pinkerton further expense. New lines were substituted in which Butterfly declares her intention to worship the same god as Pinkerton — though the music remained the same.

The major alteration made by Carré however was to the scene involving Kate Pinkerton. He removed the direct confrontation of Butterfly and Kate by keeping the American woman at a distance in the garden, and indicating by stage directions, that she should not step even onto the terrace of the house. Many of her lines he removed, either giving them to Sharpless, or providing new ones for Butterfly herself. The one move indicated for Kate in Butterfly's presence he marked 'timidly'. The orchestral music was not changed in any respect to accommodate these alterations — only the voice parts were different, but the character of Kate is totally changed in the new version. The hard, callous woman of the first version became a sympathetic and compassionate lady.

Ricordi and Puccini had to wait longer than they had expected to test Carré's version of Butterfly in practice. The rehearsal period was a depressing time for the composer. He had gone to Paris in mid-October, and, despite being in bad health, had stayed on in a city he didn't much care for in the hope that the performances would not be long delayed. He went home for a brief spell in December, returning in time for the first performance, which took place on December 28. He was enormously cheered by the success of the production, coming as it did after such a protracted and difficult rehearsal period. Strangely though, his letters do not include any comment on the viability of the new version. At some point after the Paris performances, he and Giulio Ricordi decided that the Paris version should become the standard score of *Butterfly*, with the exception of one or two minor details. Both men certainly wanted a definitive version established. In following Carré's they were certainly swayed by its success, and probably also by the argument that, if it was wise to avoid offending the special taste of Parisian audiences, it would be safer to omit the offensive elements in other theatres as well. Ricordi himself had mentioned to Puccini in an earlier letter that the scene involving Kate was difficult to bring off in its original form. Carré's version neatly side-stepped these difficulties, and at the same time provided a Pinkerton more likely to charm audiences than discomfort them.

The story does not quite end here. Shortly after the first world war a production of *Butterfly* took place at the Teatro Carcano in Milan. This small theatre was generally used for plays, but enjoyed a period of operatic activity during the war and just afterwards. The house of Ricordi have a vocal score of *Butterfly* with a note attached to it in the hand of Maestro Tenaglia, disclosing that the score represents the version of the opera as performed at the Teatro Carcano, with alterations authorised by Puccini. There are three manuscript inserts in the score, all in the first act, each restoring a section of music cut between the première in 1904 and the Paris production of 1906. The passages are the one in which Butterfly describes her uncles, that in which Yakuside gets drunk, leading into 'O Kami O Kami', and the extra section in the love duet. No other reference to Puccini's part in this production has been found.

The changes made to Puccini's opera did much more than remove the odd passage containing irrelevant detail, and the occasional hiccup in the development of the plot. The original *Butterfly* was a daring opera, unconventional in its structure, and unsparing in its delivery of what, for its time, was an unusually pointed moral and social message. The Milan audience of 1904 rejected the former, and Albert Carré, on behalf of the bourgeois Parisians, successfully diluted the latter.

The remarkable photographs of Rosina Storchio, the first Cio-Cio-San, in the movements she practised for the role. (Stuart-Liff Collection)

Madame Butterfly

John Luther Long

This magazine article first appeared in 1898 in North America, and was the source of Belasco's play. It was published in London in 1905, with other short stories by the same author.

I: Sayre's Prescription

Sayre had counselled him on the voyage out (for he had repined ceaselessly at what he called their banishment to the Asiatic station) to wait till they arrived. *He* had never regarded service in Japanese waters as banishment, he said, and he had been out twice before.

Pinkerton had just come from the Mediterranean.

'For lack of other amusement,' continued Sayre, with a laugh, 'you might get yourself married and —'

Pinkerton arrested him with a savage snort.

'You are usually merely frivolous, Sayre; but to-day you are silly.'

Without manifest offence, Sayre went on:

'When I was out here in 1890 —'

'The story of the Pink Geisha?'

'Well — yes,' admitted Sayre, patiently.

'Excuse me, then till you are through.' He turned to go below.

'Heard it, have you?'

'A thousand times — from you and others.'

Sayre laughed good-naturedly at the gallant exaggeration, and passed Pinkerton his cigarette-case.

'Ah — ever heard who the man was?'

'No.' He lighted his cigarette. 'That has been your own little mystery — apparently.'

'Apparently?'

'Yes; we all knew it was yourself.'

'It wasn't,' said Sayre, steadily. 'It was my brother.' He looked away.

'Oh!'

'He's dead.'

'Beg pardon. You never told us that.'

'He went back; couldn't find her.'

'And you advise me also to become a subject for remorse? That's good of you.'

'It is not quite the same thing. There is no danger of you losing your head for —' he glanced uncertainly at Pinkerton, then ended lamely — 'any one. The danger would probably be entirely with — the other person.'

'Thanks,' laughed Pinkerton; 'that's more comforting.'

'And yet,' mused Sayre, 'you are hard to comfort — humanly speaking.'

Pinkerton smiled at this naïve but quite exact characterisation of himself.

'You are,' continued Sayre, hesitating for the right word — 'impervious.'

'Exactly,' laughed Pinkerton. 'I *don't* see much danger to myself in your prescription. You have put it in rather an attractive light. The idea cannot be entirely disreputable if your brother Jack used it. We lower-class fellows used to call him Agamemnon, you remember.'

'It is not my prescription,' said Sayre, briefly, leaving the deck.

II: Mr B.F. Pikkerton — and His Way

But Pinkerton not only got himself married; he provided himself with an establishment — creating his menage in quite his own way and entirely for his own comfort.

With the aid of a marriage-broker, he found both a wife and a house in which to keep her. This he leased for nine hundred and ninety-nine years. Not, he explained to his wife later, that he could hope for the felicity of residing there with her so long, but because, being a mere 'barbarian', he could not make other legal terms. He did not mention that the lease was determinable, nevertheless, at the end of any month, by the mere neglect to pay the rent. Details were distasteful to Pinkerton; besides, she would probably not appreciate the humour of this.

Some clever Japanese artisans then made the paper walls of the pretty house eye-proof, and, with their own adaptations of American hardware, the openings cunningly lockable. The rest was Japanese.

Madame Butterfly laughed, and asked him why he had gone to all that trouble — in Japan!

'To keep out those who are out, and in those who are in,' he replied, with an amorous threat in her direction.

She was greatly pleased with it all, though, and went about jingling her new keys and her new authority like toys — she had only one small maid to command — until she learned that among others to be excluded were her own relatives.

There had been what her husband called an appalling horde of these at the wedding (they had come with lanterns and banners and disturbing evidences of good will), and he asked her, when she questioned him, whether she did not think they would be a trifle wearisome.

'*You* thing so?' she asked in turn.

'Emphatically,' said her husband.

She grew pale; she had not expected quite such an answer. A Japanese would have said no, but would have left an interrogation in one's mind.

He laughed consolingly.

'Well, Ane-San' (which meant only 'elder sister': there are no terms of endearment in the Japanese language), 'you will have to get along without ancestors. Think of the many people who would like to do that, and be comforted.'

'Who?' She had never heard of such a thing.

'People, for instance, whose ancestors have perished on the gallows, or, in America, have practised trades.'

She did not understand, as often she did not, and he went on:

'I shall have to serve in the capacity of ancestors — let us say ancestors-at-large — and the real ones will have to go — or rather not come.'

Again he had the joke to himself; his wife had gone away to cry.

At first she decided to run away from him. But this, she reflected, would not probably please her relatives, since they had unanimously agreed upon the marriage for her. Besides, she preferred to remain. She had acquired a strange liking for Pinkerton and her new way of life. Finally she undertook a weak remonstrance — a very strong one, in fact, for a Japanese wife; but Pinkerton encouraged her pretty domestic autonomy. Her airs of authority were charming. And they grew more and more so.

'Mr B. F. Pikkerton' — it was this, among other things, he had taught her to call him — 'I lig if you permit my august ancestors visit me. I lig ver' *moach* if you *please* permit that unto me.'

Her hair had been newly dressed for the occasion, and she had stuck a poppy in it. Besides, she put her hand on his arm (a brave thing for her to do), and smiled wistfully up at him. And when you know what Cho-Cho-San's smile was like — and her hand — and its touch — you will wonder how Pinkerton resisted her. However, he only laughed at her — good-naturedly always — and said no.

'We can't adopt a whole regiment of back numbers, you know. You are back number enough for me.'

And though he kissed her, she went away and cried again; and Japanese girls do not often cry.

He could not understand how important this concession was to her. It must be confessed that he did not try to understand. Sayre, with a little partisanship, explained to him that in Japan filial affection is the paramount motive, and that these 'ancestors', living and dead, were his wife's sole link to such eternal life as she hoped for. He trusted that Pinkerton would not forget this.

He would provide her a new motive, then, Pinkerton said — perhaps meaning himself, — and a new religion, if she *must* have one — himself again. So when she, at his motion, diffidently undertook to clothe on the phantoms which made up her 'religion', Pinkerton expounded what he called the easier Western plan of salvation — seriously, too, considering that all his communications to her were touched with whimsy. This was inevitable — to Pinkerton. After all, she *was* quite an impossible little thing, outside of lacquer and paint. But he struck deeper than he knew; for she went secretly to the church of the missionary who served on the opposite hill, and heard the same thing, and learned, moreover, that she might adopt this new religion at any time she chose — even the eleventh hour.

She went out joyously; not to adopt his religion, it is true, but to hold it in reserve if her relatives should remain obdurate. Pinkerton, to his relief, heard no more of it.

III: A Moon-Goddess Truly

But his wife's family (the word has a more important application there than here) held a solemn conference, and, as the result of it, certain of them waited upon Lieutenant Pinkerton, and, with elaborate politeness, intimated that his course had theretofore been quite unknown in Japan. This was their oblique way of saying that it was unsatisfactory. They pointed out with patient gravity that he would thus limit his wife's opportunities of reappearing on earth in a higher form of life.

Pinkerton smilingly remarked that he was not sure that it would be best for his wife to reappear on earth in a higher form. She would probably accomplish mischief enough in this very charming one — as she was in fact doing.

'Do you know,' he continued to the spokesman, 'that you look exactly like a lacquered tragedy mask I have hanging over my desk?'

One must have seen one of these masks to appreciate this.

But they all laughed good-naturedly, as their host had designed, and quite forgot their errand. And Pinkerton laboured that they should remember it no more. This was quite Japanese. In the politest way possible he made them drink his liquors and smoke his tobacco (in the generous Western fashion),

The arrival of the Bonze in the 1945 Sadler's Wells production with Victoria Sladen as Cio-Cio-San, Valetta Jacopi as Suzuki, Arthur Servent as Pinkerton, Roderick Jones as Sharpless and Rhys Williams as Goro (photo: Angus McBean, © Harvard Theatre Collection)

either of which operations was certain to make a Japanese very ill. This was thoroughly like Pinkerton.

They protested a deal of friendship for Pinkerton that night; but at the final conference, where Cho-Cho-San was solemnly disowned, none were more gloomily unfriendly than they who had eaten and drunken with him.

'I did the very best I could for you, little moon-goddess,' said Pinkerton to his wife; 'but they were proof against my best wine and tobacco.'

She bent her head in reflection a moment.

'Ah, you mean — I begin learn you, Mr B.F. Pikkerton! You mean they *not* proof. Aha!'

And Pinkerton delightedly embraced her.

'You are no longer a back number,' he said.

'Aha! Tha' 's what *I* thing. Now I bed you I know what *is* that bag nomber!'

'Well?'

'People lig I *was*.'

'Exactly.'

'But not people lig I *am*?'

'No; you are up-to-date.'

'I egspeg I ought be sawry?' She sighed hypocritically.

'Exactly why, my moon-maid?'

'Account they outcasting me. Aeverybody thing me mos' bes' wicked in all Japan. Nobody speak to me no more — they all outcast me *aex*cep' jus' you; that' 's why I ought be sawry.'

She burst into a reckless laugh, and threw herself like a child upon him.

'But tha' 's ezag' why I am *not*! Wha' 's use lie? It is not inside me — that sawry. Me? I'm mos' bes' happy female woman in Japan — mebby in that whole worl'. What you thing?'

He said honestly that he thought she was, and he took honest credit for it.

IV: Trouble — Meaning Joy

And after his going, in the whimsical delight they had practised together, she named the baby, when it came, Trouble. Every Japanese baby begins with a temporary name; it may be anything, almost, for the little time. She was quite sure he would like the way she had named him Trouble — meaning joy. That was his own oblique way. As for his permanent name — he might have several others before — that was for him to choose when he returned. And this event was to happen, according to his own words, when the robins nested again.

And spring and the robins had come.

All this to explain why Madame Butterfly and her baby were reclining on the immaculate mats in attitudes of artistic abandon, instead of keeping an august state, as all other Japanese mothers and babies were at this moment doing. American women, we are told, assume more fearless attitudes in the security of their boudoirs than elsewhere. Japanese women, never. Their conduct is eternally the same. It must be as if someone were looking on — always. There is no privacy for them short of the grave. They have no secure boudoirs.

But Madame Butterfly (through the courtesy of her American husband) had both these. It will therefore be argued, perhaps, that she is not a typical Japanese woman. But it is only Lieutenant Pinkerton's views about which we are presently concerned. He called her an American refinement of a Japanese product, an American improvement in a Japanese invention, and so on. And since he knew her best, his words concerning her should have a certain ex-cathedra authority. I know no more.

And she and the maid, and the baby too, were discussing precisely the matters which have interested us hitherto — Pinkerton, his baby, his imminent return, etc..

Cho-Cho-San, with a deft jerk that was also a caress, brought the baby into her lap as she sat suddenly up.

'Ah, *you* — you think he is just like any other baby. But — he is a miracle! Yes!' she insisted belligerently. 'The Sun-Goddess sent him straight from the Bridge of Heaven! Because of those prayers so early — oh, so *very* early — in the morning. Oh, that is the time to pray!' She turned the baby violently so that she might see his eyes. 'Now did anyone *ever* hear of a Japanese baby with purple eyes?'

She held him over against the dwarfed wistaria which grew in a flat bronze koro at the tokonoma, full of purple blossoms. She addressed the maid Suzuki, who stood by, happy as herself, apparently aware that this subject must always be discussed vehemently.

'As purple as that! Answer me, thou giggler; is it not so? Speak! I *will* have an answer!'

Then the maid laughed out a joyous no. If she cherished the Eastern reservations concerning blue eyes and pink cheeks, it was a less heinous offence to lie about it a little than to assert it impolitely. Besides, neither she nor anyone else could resist the spirits of her pretty mistress. And these spirits had grown joyously riotous since her marriage and its unfettering.

'Nor yet so bald of his head? Say so! Quickly!' she insisted, with the manner of Pinkerton — such is example!

The maid also agreed to this.

And then Cho-Cho-San flung the kicking youngster high above her, turned abandonedly over on her back (in charming, if forbidden, postures), and juggled with him there.

'But ah! you *will* have hair, will you not? — as long and glittering as that of the American women. I will not endure thee else.' She became speciously savage. 'Speak, thou beggar, speak!'

'Goo-goo,' said the baby, endeavouring diligently to obey.

She shook him threateningly.

'Ah-h-h! You making that non-*senze* with your parent? Now what *is* that you speaking with me? Jap'nese? If it is, I —' She threatened him direly. But he had evidently already learned to understand her; he gurgled again. 'Listen! *No* one shall speak anything but United States' languages in these house! *Now*! What you thing? You go'n' go right outside shoji firs' thing you do that!' She resumed her own English more ostentatiously — she forgot it herself sometimes — and pretended to pitch the baby through the fragile paper wall.

'Also, tha' 's one thing *aevery*body got recomlek — account it is his house, his wife, his bebby, his maiden, his moaney — oh — *aevery*thing is his! An' he say, those time he go'n' 'way, that *aex*cep' we all talking those United States' languages when he come, he go'n' bounce us all. *Well*! I don' git myself bounce, Mr Trouble! An' you got loog out you don', aha! Sa-*ay*, me? I thing if we doing all those thing he as' us, he go'n' take us at those United States America, an' live in his castle. Then he never *kin* bounce us, aha!'

V: A Song of Sorrow — and Death — and Heaven

A bird flew to the vine in the little porch.

'Ah, Suzuki!'

But the maid had withdrawn. She clapped her hands violently for her to return.

'Now why *do* you go away when' — her momentary anger fled, and she laughed — 'when birds flying to the wistaria? Go quickly, little maiden, and see if he is a robin, and if he has completed his nest — quickly.'

The maid returned, and said that he was indeed a robin, but that he had no nest there as yet.

'Oh, *how* he is slow! Suzuki, let us fine 'nother robin, one that is more industri-ous — an' domes-tic, aha, ha ha!'

'They are all alike,' said the girl, cynically.

'They — *not*! Say so!'

Suzuki giggled affirmatively. When her mistress took so violently to

Minnie Nast, who created the role of Sophie in 'Der Rosenkavalier' in Dresden, as Cio-Cio-San (Stuart-Liff Collection)

English she preferred to express herself in this truly Japanese fashion.

'Inform me, if you please, how much nearer beggary we are to-day than yesterday, Suzuki.'

The girl had exact information for her on this subject. She said they had just seventeen yen, fifty-four sen, two rin.

'Alas — alas! *How* we have waste his beau-tiful moaneys! Tha' 's shame. *But* he will not permit that we starve — account he know we have no one *aex*cep' him. We all outcasted. Now loog *how* that is bad! *So*, jus' when it is all gone he will come with more — lig the stories of ole Kazabu. *Oh*! lig story of Uncombed Ronin, who make a large oath that he go'n' be huge foo-el if he dress his hair until his lord arrive back from the banishment. *Lo*! when they cutting his hade off him, account he don' comb his hair, his lord arrive back, an' say, "What they doing with him?" — an' reward him great deal, account he constant ontil he 'mos' dead. *So*, jus' when we go'n' out on the street — mebby to fine him — you with Trouble on your back, me with my samisen, standing up bifore all the people, singing funeral songs, with faces, oh, 'bout 'mos' so long' — she illustrated liberally — 'sad garments, hair all ruffled — so, dancing liddle — so' — she indicated how she should dance — 'an' saying out ver' loud, "O ye people! Listen, for the loave of all the eight hundred thousan' gods and goddesses! Behole, we, a poor widow, an' a bebby what got purple eyes, which had one hosban', which gone off at United States America, to naever return no more *naever*! *Aex*cep' you have seen him? No? See! This what I thing. Oh, how that is mos' tarrible! We giving up all our august ancestors, an' gods, an' people, an' country — oh *aevery*thing — jus' for him, an' now he don' naever come no more! Oh, *how* that is sad! Is it not? Also, he don' even divorce us, so that we kin marry with 'nother mans an' git some food. *He*? He don' even *thing* 'bout it! Not liddle bit! He forgitting us — alas! *But* we got keep his house nine hundred an' ninety-nine year! Now thing 'bout *that*! An' we go'n' starve bifore, *aex*cep' you giving us — ah-ah--*ah*! jus' one sen! two sen! mebby fi' sen! Oh, for the loave of sorrow, for the loave of constancy, for the loave of death, jus' — one — sen! Will you please pity us? In the name of the merciful Kwannon we beg. Loog! To move your hearts in the inside you, we go'n' sing you a song of — sorrow — an' death — an' heaven."'

She had acted it all with superb spirit, and now she snatched up her samisen, and dramatised this also; and so sure was she of life and happiness that this is the song of sorrow and death she sang:

'Hikari nodokeki haru no nobe,
Niwo sakura-no-hana sakari,
Mure kuru hito no tanoshiki ni,
Shibashi uki yo ya wasururan.

'Sunshine on a quiet plain in spring,
The perfume of the blooming cherry-blossoms,
The joy of the gathering crowd,
Filled with love, forget the care of life.'

And then, as always, abandonment and laughter.

'Aha, ha, ha! Aha, ha, ha! What you thing, liddle maiden? Tha' 's good song 'bout sorrow, an' death, an' heaven? Aha, ha, ha! What — you — thing? Speak! Say so!

She tossed the samisen to its place, and sprang savagely at the maid.

'If that Mr B.F. Pikkerton see us doing alig those —' ventured the maid, in the humour of her mistress.

'O-o-o! You see his eye flame an' scorch lig lightening! O-o-o! He snatch us away to the house — so — so — *so*!'

The baby was the unfortunate subject for the illustration of this. He began to whimper.

'Rog-a-by, bebby, off in Japan,
You jus' a picture off of a fan.'

This was from Pinkerton. She had been the baby then.

'Ah, liddle beggar, he di'n' know he go'n' make those poetries for you! He don' suspect of you whichever. *Well*! I bed you we go'n' have some fun when he *do*. Oh, Suzuki! Some day, when the emperor go abroad, we will show him. You got say these way' — she changed her voice to what she fancied an impressive male basso: '"Behole, Heaven-Descended-Ruler-Everlasting-Great-Japan, the first of your subjecks taken his eye out those ver' blue heaven whence you are descend!" Hence the emperor loog on him; then he *stop* an' loog; he kin naever git enough loogs. Then he make Trouble a large prince! An' me? He jus' say onto me: "Continue that you bring out such sons." Aha, ha, ha! What you thing?'

The maid was frankly sceptical.

'At least you kin do lig the old nakodo wish you — for you are most beautiful.'

Cho-Cho-San dropped the baby with a reckless thud, and sprang at her again. She gripped her throat viciously, then flung her, laughing, aside.

'Speak concerning marriage once more, an' you die. An' tha' 's 'nother thing. You got know at his United States America, if one is marry one got stay marry — oh, for aever an' aever! *Yaes*! Nob'y cannot git himself divorce, *aex*cep' in a large court-house an' jail. Tha' 's way with he — that Mr B.F. Pikkerton — an' me — that Mrs B.F. Pikkerton. If he aever go'n' divorce me, he got take me at those large jail at that United States America. Tha' 's lot of trouble; hence he rather stay marry with me. Also, he *lig* be marry with me. Now loog! He leave me a 'mos' largest lot money in Japan; he give me his house for live inside for nine hundred an' ninety-nine year. I cannot go home at my grandmother, account he make them outcast me. Sa-*ay*, you liddle foolish! He coming when the robins nest again. Aha! What you thing? Say so!'

The maid should have been excused for not being always as recklessly jubilant as her mistress; but she never was. And now, when she chose silence rather than speech (which was both more prudent and more polite), she took it very ill.

VI: Divine Foolery

If Pinkerton had told her to go home, even though she had no home to go to, she would have been divorced without more ado. Perhaps she was logical (for she reasoned as he had taught her — she had never reasoned before) in considering that as he had distinctly told her not to do so, it was an additional surety for his return.

Cho-Cho-San again took up the happier side of the matter. The baby was asleep.

'An' also, what you thing we bedder doing when he come?'

She was less forcible now, because less certain. This required planning to get the utmost felicity out of it — what she always strove for.

'Me? — I thing I — dun*no*,' the maid confessed diplomatically.

'Aha, ha, ha! You dun*no*? Of course you dunno whichever! Well — I go'n' tell you.' The plan had been born and matured that instant in her active little brain. 'Jus' recomleck 't is a secret among you an' me. We don' tell that Mr. Trouble. Hoash! He don' kin keep no secret. *Well*, listen! We go'n' watch with that spying-glass till his ship git in. Then we go' n' put cherry-blossoms aeverywhere; an' if 't is night, we go'n' hang up 'bout 'most one thousan' lanterns — 'bout 'most one thousan'! Then we — *wait*. Jus' when we see him coming up that hill — so — so — so — *so*' — she lifted her kimono, and strode masculinely about the apartment — 'then! We hide behine the shoji, where there are holes to peep.' She glanced about to find them. 'Alas! they all mended shut! *But*' — she savagely ran her finger through the paper — 'we soon make some, aha, ha, ha! So!' She made another for the maid. They illustrated this phase of her mood with their eyes at the holes. 'Then we lie quiet lig mice, an' make believe we gone 'way. Better n't we leave liddle note: "Gone 'way foraever. Sayonara, Butterfly"? No; tha' 's too long for him. He git angery those ways on the first word, an' say those remark 'bout debbil, an' hell, an' all kind loud languages. Tha' 's time, bifore he gitting *too* angery, to rush out, an' jump all rou' his neck, aha!' This was also illustrated.

But, alas! the maid was too realistic.

'Sa-*ay*! not *you* — jump roun' his neck — jus' *me*.'

Cho-Cho-San paused ecstatically. But the maid would not have it so. She had seen them practise such divine foolery — very like two reckless children — but never had she seen anything with such dramatic promise as this.

'Oh! an' what he say *then*,' she begged, with wild interest, 'an' what he *do*?'

Madame Butterfly was re-energised by the maid's applause.

'Ah-h-h!' she sighed. 'He don' *say* — jus' he *kiss* us, oh, 'bout three — seven — ten — a thousan' time! An' amberace us two thousan' time 'bout 'mos' — tha' 's what he *do* — till we got make him stop, aha, ha, ha! account he might — might — *kill* us! Tha' 's *ver*' bad — to be kill kissing.'

Her extravagant mood infected the maid. She had long ago begun to wonder whether, after all, this American passion of affection was altogether despicable. She remembered that her mistress had begun by regarding it thus; yet now she was the most daringly happy woman in Japan.

'Say more,' the maid pleaded.

Cho-Cho-San had a fine fancy, and the nesting of the robins could not, at the longest, be much longer delayed now; she let it riot.

'Well' — she was making it up as she went — 'when tha' 's all done, he loog roun' those ways lig he doing 'mos' always, an' he see sump'n', an' he say: "Oh, 'el-*lo* — *el*-lo! Where you got that chile?" I say: "Ah — oh — *ah*! I thing mebby you lig own one, an' I buy 'im of a man what din' wan' no bebby with those purple eye an' bald hairs." An' he as' me, "What you pay?" Americans always as' what you pay. I say: "Oh, lemme see. I thing, two yen an' two sen. Tha' 's too moach for bald bebby?" What you thing? But tha' 's a time he saying: "I bed you tha' 's a liar; an' you fooling among me." Then he gitting angery, an' I hurry an' say, one las' time, "Tha' 's right. I tole you liddle lie for a *fun*. I di'n' pay *naw*thing for him, *aex*cep' — sa-*ay*! —" Then I whisper a thing inside his ear — jus' a liddle thing — an' he *see*! Aha, ha, ha! Then he say once more, las' time — ah, what you thing, Suzuki?'

But the girl would not diminish her pleasure by guessing.

'"*God*amighty!" Aha, ha, ha!'

'Tha' 's all things you know?' questioned the maid, reproachfully, 'an' all things you do?'

She had a right to feel that she had been defrauded out of a proper dénouement.

'Ah-h-h-h! What would you have that is more? Jus' joy an' glory foraevermore! Tha' 's 'nough. What you thing? You know that song?

''Tis life when we meet,
'Tis death when we part.'

Her mistress had grown plaintive in those two lines.

'I hear him sing that,' murmured the maid, comfortingly.

Her spirits vaulted up again.

'But ah! You aever hear him sing —?'

She snatched up the samisen again, and to its accompaniment sang, in the pretty jargon he had taught her (making it as grotesque as possible, the more to amuse him):

'I call her the belle of Japan — of Japan;
Her name it is O Cho-Cho-San — Cho-Cho-San;
Such tenderness lies in her soft almond eyes,
I tell you she's just ichi ban.'

Tamaki Miura, the first Japanese-born singer to make an international career. She made her London debut as Cio-Cio-San in 1915 at the London Opera House, and performed the title role in Messager's 'Madame Chrysanthème' in Chicago in 1920. (Stuart-Liff Collection)

'Tha' 's *me* — aha, ha, ha! Sa-*ay* — you thing he aever going away again when he got that liddle chile, an' the samisen, an' the songs, an' all the joy, an' — an' *me*?' And another richly joyous laugh.

'Oh, you an' the samisen an' joy — poof!' said the maid. 'But the chile — tha' 's 'nother kind thing. *Aex*cep' *he* grow up, an' go 'way after his father?'

She was odiously unsatisfied. She would leave nothing to fate — to heaven — Shaka. But out of her joyous future her mistress satisfied even this grisly doubt.

'Ah-h-h! *But* we go'n' have *more* — lig steps of a ladder, up, up, up! An' all purple eyes — oh, aevery one! An' all males! Then, if one go 'way, we got 'nother an' 'nother an' 'nother. Then, how *kin* he, that Mr B.F. Pikkerton, *aever* go 'way? Aha!'

'Yaet, O Cho-Cho-San, if you —'

Was this a new doubt? It will never be known.

'Stop! Tha' 's 'nother thing. You got call me O Cho-Cho-San, *an'* Missus Ben-ja-meen Frang-a-leen Pikkerton. Sa-*ay*; you notize how that soun' gran' when my hosban' speaking it that aways? Yaes! 'Mos' lig I was a emperess. Listen! I tell you 'nother thing, which is 'nother secret among you an' me jus': I thing it is more nize to be call that away — jus' Missus Ben-ja-meen Frang-a-leen Pikkerton — than Heaven-Descended-Female-Ruler-Everlasting-Great-Japan, aha! Sa*ay*; how I loog if I an emperess? What you thing?'

She imitated the pose and expression of her empress very well.

'If you face liddle longer you loog ezag' lig,' said the maid.

But her mistress was inclined to be more modest.

'Ah, no. *But* I tell you who loog lig a' emperor — jus' ezag' — that Mr B.F. Pikkerton, when he got that unicorn upon him, with gole all up in front an' down behine!'

And at this gentle treason there was no protest from the patriotic maid.

VII: How He Didn't Understand Her Whichever!

The baby continued to sleep. He rather justified the praises of his mother. He was as good as a Japanese baby, and as good-looking as an American one.

Somebody was without. There was a polite and subdued clattering of clogs in the entrance.

'Gomen nasai' ('I beg your pardon').

It was a familiar, deprecatory voice, accompanied by the clapping of hands.

Cho-Cho-San smiled wearily, and called the maid.

'Oh, Suzuki, Goro the nakodo — he is without. Shaka and all the gods defend us now!'

The two exchanged glances of amusement, and the maid proceeded to admit him.

Madame Butterfly received him with the odious lack of ceremony her independent life with Pinkerton had bred. She was imperially indifferent. The go-between pointed out how sad this was to as beautiful a woman as she.

'Is it a trouble to you?' she asked, perking her head aside.

The nakodo only sighed gloomily.

Madame Butterfly laughed.

'Poor, nize liddle ole man,' said she, with specious pity, in politest English; 'do not trouble 'bout me. Do not arrive any more if it pains you.'

'I must; you have no parents now — nor anyone. You are outcast.'

'Ah-h-h! *But*, will you not permit *me* to suffer the lack?'

'But you will never be married!'

'Again?'

'Well — yes, again, then.'

'How tarrible!'

He took this quite seriously, and became more cheerful.

'Yes; a beautiful woman like you must have a husband.'

'Yaes. Thangs; I got *one*. Do you perhaps mean more?'

'I mean a Japanese husband.'

'Oh — ah? That will have me a month, and then divorce me? And then another, and another, and another?'

She was becoming belligerent.

'How is it better with you now?'

She recovered her good humour.

'At America one is married foraever — *aex*cep' the other die. Aha! What you thing? Your marriages are not so.'

She had been speaking indifferently both languages, and now the nakodo, who was not apt at English, begged her to explain this in Japanese. She did so.

'Yamadori has lived long at America, and he says it is not thus. Is it not safe to rely upon his excellent wisdom?'

'No; for I, which am foolish, are wiser than both you an' he. *I* know. You jus' guess. Aeverybody got stay marry at United States America. No one can git divorce, *aex*cep' he stay in a large court-house, all full judges with long faces, an' bald on their heads, long, long time; mebby two — four — seven year! Now jus' thing 'bout that — *how* that is tiresome! Tha' 's why no one don' git no divorce; they too tire' to wait. Firs', the man he got go an stan' bifore those judge, an' tell all he thing 'bout it. Then the woman she got. Then some lawyers quarrel with those judge; an' then the judges git jury, an' as' 'em what they thing 'bout it; an' if they don' know they *all* git put in jail till they git done thinging 'bout it, an' whether they go'n' git divorce or not. Aha!'

'Where did you learn that?' asked the old nakodo, aghast.

'Oh — ah — that Mr B.F. Pikkerton' — she assumed a grander air — 'That Mr Ben-ja-meen Frang-a-leen Pikkerton — my hosban' —' She smiled engagingly, and held out her pretty hands, as who should say: 'Is not *that* sufficient?'

It was so evidently the invention of Pinkerton that it seemed superfluous to make the explanation. The nakodo said curtly that he did not believe it.

Not believe what Mr B.F. Pinkerton had said!

Cho-Cho-San was exasperated. The engaging smile had been wasted. She flung the blue-eyed baby up before him.

'Well, then, do you believe *that*?'

She laughed almost malignantly. The marriage-broker gulped down this fearful indignity as best he might. He hoped there were not going to be any more such women in Japan as the result of foreign marriages. Still, even this phase of the situation had been discussed with his client.

'But Yamadori, who was bred to the law, tells me that our law prevails in such a matter, the marriage having taken place here.'

She gave a gasp, and cried like a savage wounded animal:

'Yamadori — lies!'

The nakodo was silenced. She crushed the baby so fiercely to her breast that he began to cry.

'*Sh!*' she commanded harshly. He looked up for an incredulous instant, then burrowed his head affrightedly into her kimono. She turned upon the nakodo in magnificent scorn.

'Oh — *you* — *foo-el*! You thing he naever arrive back. Tha' 's what you thing — in secret! He? He *do*!'

She snatched a photograph from an easel at the tokonoma, tore the child from his hiding, and held them up together. Her purpose was quite evident.

The nakodo was thoroughly frightened. She recovered her poise — and her control of the situation.

'*Now* what you thing? Aha, ha, ha! Sa-*ay* — I bed you all moaneys he go'n' come 'mos' one millions mile for see that chile! Tha' 's what I all times praying Shaka an' the augustnesses for — one chile ezag' lig him. *Well*, sa-*ay*! I got him. An' now that Mr Ben-ja-meen Frang-a-leen Pikkerton he *got* come back — hoarry — even if he don' lig. He cannot stand it. But he do lig.'

All her passion was gone now, and her sure gladness returned. She was naïve and intimate and confidential again.

'Sa-*ay*! Firs' I pray his large American God, — that huge Godamighty, — but tha' 's no use. He don' know me where I live. Then I pray Shaka an' all the kaimyo of the augustnesses in the god-house. I thing they don' hear me, account they outcasted me when I marry with that Mr B.F. Pikkerton. *But*' — she smiled at her pretty celestial cajolery — 'I pray them so long an'

Magdalena Falewicz as Cio-Cio-San and Julian Moyle as Prince Yamadori (seated) in Joachim Herz's production for Welsh National Opera, 1980 (photo: Julian Sheppard)

so moach more than they aever been pray with bifore that they feel good all times, an' — an" — there was finality in this — 'an' 't *is* use. An' mebby I not *all* outcasted! Don' tell him. He — he laugh upon my gods, an' say they jus' wood an' got no works in them. An' he all times call the augustnesses bag nombers! Jus' he don' know till he fine out. Aha, ha, ha!'

'If he returns he will probably take the child away with him — that is his right,' chanted the sad-faced nakodo.

But nothing could ruffle Madame Butterfly now. She laughed sibilantly at this owl-like ignorance.

'Oh-h-h! *How* you don' know things! *How* you don' onderstan' me what I mean, whichever! Of course he take that chile away with him — of course! An' *me* — me also; an' Suzuki, aha! An' we go an' live in his castle for aever an' aever!'

The improbability of changing the girl's point of view began to dawn upon the slow intellect of the nakodo.

'At least, Yamadori wishes for a look-at meeting. I have promised him. Will you not grant this?'

Cho-Cho-San shook her head at him knowingly.

'An' if I do not, he not go'n' pay you one present?'

She laughed wildly, and the nakodo by a grin admitted the impeachment.

'Well' — the spirit of mischief possessed the girl — 'sa-*ay* — I don' keer. Let him come. He lig for see me; I lig for see him. An' if I say I go'n' marry him, he got hoarry an' marry me right away. Aha! What you thing 'bout *those*?'

The nakodo said delightedly that that was precisely what he sought.

'Yaes; *but* suppose they put me in a large jail, an' got loog out between bar — so' — she illustrated — 'an' don' git nawthing for eat; he go'n' stay all times behine my side, an' comforting me? Hol' my hand? Lemme weep upon him? I dun*no*. Mebby they cut my hade off me. Then he got git his hade cut off, too, an' go the road to Meido together — with — without those hade! Oh, *how* that is tarrible! An' suppose' — she whispered it horridly — 'that Mr B.F. Pikkerton — aha, ha, ha! — *arrive*?'

The nakodo was not sure how much of this was meant seriously. They were extremely unusual humours to him. But she had consented to the meeting, and he promptly took her at her word.

'When, then, will it please you to have me bring Yamadori?'

'When you lig — nize liddle ole friend.'

The nakodo fixed that day a week.

As he was going, Cho-Cho-San laughingly asked:

'Sa-*ay*! How often he been marry?'

'But twice,' the nakodo replied virtuously.

'An' both times divorce?'

He admitted that this was the case.

'An' both times jus' on visit from United States America — jus' *liddle* visit? — so long?' she spread her hands.

Under her laughing gaze it seemed best to admit it.

'Oh! *he* — he jus' marry 'nother for *fun* — whenever he thing 'bout it. Then he forgit it when he don' thing 'bout it, and marry 'nother. Say so!'

He heard her laugh again as he left the courtyard; but he had confidence in the ability of Yamadori to accomplish his purpose if he could be brought into contact with her. He was one of the modern pensioned princes of Japan, a desirable matrimonial article, and preternaturally fascinating.

VIII: The Bright-Red Spot in Cho's Cheeks

The look-at meeting came about as planned. There was a distinct air of state about Madame Butterfly's house on that day. The baby, and all the frivolities that attended him, were in banishment. The apartment had been enlarged by the rearrangement of the shoji. At the head of it, statuesque in her most brilliant attire, sat Cho-Cho-San. Japanese women are accomplished actresses; and looking in upon Cho-Cho-San just at the moment of Yamadori's arrival, one would not have known her. She was as unsmiling, as emotionless, as the Dai-Butsu.

The grave ceremonies attending the advent of a candidate for matrimony went forward with almost no recognition from Cho-Cho-San until they had come to the point where they might seat themselves before her, to inspect and be inspected. Then she struck her fan against her palm, and Suzuki appeared, and set the tobacco-bon between them.

Yamadori suggested somewhat the ready-made clothier — inevitable evidence of his transformation; otherwise he was the average modern Japanese, with high-gibbeted trousers, high collar, high hat, and eye-glass. He might not converse directly with Cho-Cho-San, especially concerning the business in hand; but he was not prohibited from conferring with the nakodo about it in her presence. The rule of decorum for such an occasion simply decreed that she should be blind and deaf concerning what went on. The convenience of the arrangement is obvious. The nakodo, the representative of both parties, was happily permitted, on the part of one, to regard what was happening as if it had not happened, and, on the part of the other, as if it had.

'She is quite as beautiful as you said,' remarked Yamadori, after a careful inspection with his glass.

The nakodo nodded virtuously, and filled his pipe. His client lighted a cigarette.

Cho-Cho-San did not even smile.

'And her father, you say, was on the emperor's side in the Satsuma rebellion?'

The marriage-broker satisfied his client to the last particular of her father's bloody sacrificial end at Jokoji.

'And you have told her faithfully of *me*?' He paused on the last word to note its effect upon Cho-Cho-San. There was none, and he hastened to add cumulatively, 'And my august family?' He paused again. But again there was no sign from the lady of the house. She was staring out over his head. 'And have offered her my miserable presents?'

To each of these the broker answered lugubriously yes.

'Then why, in the name of the gods, does she wait?'

The nakodo explained with a sigh that she had declined his presents.

'I will send her others. They shall be a thousand times more valuable. Since I have seen her I know that the first must have been an affront.'

She kept her eyes up, but Yamadori unquestionably smiled in the direction of Cho-Cho-San — as if she were a woman of joy!

The light of battle came into the stony eyes of the girl. She clapped her hands almost viciously. The little maid appeared.

'Tea!' she said.

The maid brought the tea; and with that splendid light of danger still in her eyes, Cho-Cho-San served it. With the air of a princess she put on in an instant all the charms of a mousmee. She gave back smile for smile now, and jest for jest. She begged Yamadori, with the most charming upward inflections, to put away his cigarette and take her shippo pipe, and he did it. *That* was Japanese, she said, her cigarettes were not. Was it not so? — with a resistless movement toward him. She let him touch her hands in the passage of the cups. She enveloped him with the perfume of her garments. She possessed him wholly in one dizzy instant.

'I will give her a castle to live in,' said Yamadori, breathlessly.

The nakodo sighed. Cho-Cho-San refilled his pipe with an incomparable grace.

'Ah!' she permitted her lips to breathe — very softly.

'She shall have a thousand servants.'

There was no audible response from the nakodo, but his eyes gleamed avidly.

Cho-Cho-San returned the pipe, smiling dazzlingly. It seemed almost yes with her.

'Everything her heart can wish!' cried Yamadori, recklessly.

The nakodo turned beseechingly toward the girl. She lifted her eyebrows. He did not understand. As she passed him she laughed.

'Is it enough?'

Still he did not understand.

'Have we earned the present?' she whispered.

'I will give a solemn writing,' added Yamadori, fervidly.

'She still fancies herself perhaps married to the American,' sighed the nakodo.

Yamadori laughed disagreeably.

'If your Excellency would condescend to explain —'

'Oh, she is not serious. A sailor has a sweetheart in every port, you know.'

Elisabeth Schwarzkopf as Cio-Cio-San at Covent Garden in 1950 (Royal Opera House Archives)

Cho-Cho-San whispered something to the nakodo. She still smiled.

'But she is perhaps his *wife*,' answered he, obediently.

'Yes,' said Yamadori, as if they were the same.

Cho-Cho-San whispered again.

'But the child – there is a most accomplished child?' said the nakodo.

'Yes,' said the travelled Japanese, with the same smile and the same intonation.

There was a distinct silence. Cho-Cho-San smiled more vividly. But her nostrils moved rapidly in and out. The nakodo grew anxious. Yamadori cast his eyes toward the ceiling, and continued:

'A sailor does not know the difference. In no other country are children esteemed as they are here. In America it is different. People sometimes deny them. They are left in a basket at some other person's door. But the person does not receive them. They are then cared for by the municipality as waifs. It is shameful to be such a child. There are great houses and many officers in each city for the care of these. They are an odious class by themselves, and can never rise above their first condition.'

The nakodo glanced askance at his client. He had not the slightest objection to a man who would lie a little to win his cause, but to lie too much was to lose it.

'I myself knew a man whose child became a cripple. He sent him to the mayor of the city, saying that as the cars of the city had injured him, the city must bring him up. He was sent to the poorhouse, and afterwards to the stone-quarries. It was a most piteous sight.'

Cho-Cho-San bent again to the ear of the old man. There was a tremor in her voice now.

'Had he eyes of purple?' asked the nakodo.

'He was beautiful of face; but surely eyes of purple are not desirable?' Yamadori brought his own down from the ceiling and levelled them at Cho-Cho-San. She still smiled, but there was a bright-red spot in each cheek now. 'But he was misshapen, and he was never known to laugh. I saw many such. I saw a child whose father had deserted it, and the mother —'

Madame Butterfly clapped her hands again. The maid appeared promptly; she had expected the summons.

'Suzuki — good Suzuki, the excellent gentlemen — the august' — she swept a royal gesture toward them — 'who have done us the honour to call, they wish to go hurriedly. Their shoes — will you not hasten them?'

With a final brilliant smile she turned her back upon them and left the room.

'Your story of the rejected child did it,' reproached the nakodo, on the way.

'I had not got to the worst,' said his client, ruefully. 'I meant to cite an example exactly to suit her own case.'

'Lucky she turned us out when she did, then.'

'What do you mean, sir?' demanded the suitor, in sudden wrath.

'Oh,' said the broker, in polite haste, 'I was beginning to feel — ill.'

The irony of this escaped the client. Still, Goro would have had a less opinion of Yamadori if, having lied once, he had not lied again in defence of the first.

Though Yamadori came no more, he had brought the serpent to Madame Butterfly's Eden.

IX: ''Bout Birds'

One day she took her courage, and the maid's too, for that matter, in both hands, and called upon the American consul. She saw the vice-consul. There was a west wind, and it was warm at Nagasaki. He was dozing. When he woke, Madame Butterfly was bowing before him. At a little distance was the maid with the blond baby strapped to her back. He was unable to account for them immediately.

'Goon night,' said Cho-Cho-San, smiling amiably.

The consul glanced apprehensively about.

'Night! Not night, is it?'

They both discovererd the error at the same instant.

'Ah! no, no, no! Tha' 's *mis*-take. Me — I'm liddle raddle'. Aexcuse us. Tha' 's not nize, mak' *mis*-take. We got call you good morning, I egspeg, or how do? What you thing?'

'Whichever you like,' he answered, without a smile.

Then Cho-Cho-San waited for something further from the consul. Nothing came. She began to suspect that it was her business to proceed instead of his.

'I — I thing mebby you don' know me?' she questioned, to give him a chance.

'Oh, yes, I do,' declared the consul. In fact, everybody knew her, for one reason and another — her baby, her disowning, her beauty, her 'American' marriage. 'You are O Cho-Cho-San, the daughter —' he forgot her father's name, though he had often heard it. 'You used to dance, did you not?'

'Aha! See! Tha' 's what I thing. You don' know me whichaever. I nobody's daughter; jus' Missus Ben-ja — no! Missus Frang-a-leen Ben-ja-meen —

no, no, *no*! Missus Ben-ja-meen Frang-a-leen Pikkerton. Aeverybody else outcast me. Aha, ha, ha! I liddle more raddle'.'

'Oh!' The consul was genuinely surprised, and for the first time looked with interest at the child. Cho-Cho-San, to aid him, took Trouble from the maid. Finally he politely asked her what he could do for her.

'I got as' you a thing.'

She returned the baby to the maid.

'Proceed,' said the consul.

'You know 'bout birds in your country?'

'Yes, something.'

'Ah! tha' 's what I thing. You know *aevery*thing. Tha' 's why your country sen' you here — account you ver' wise.'

'You do me too much honour,' laughed the consul.

Enrico de Franceschi as Sharpless at La Scala in 1938 (Stuart-Liff Collection)

'You — *don'* — know?'

She was distinctly alarmed.

'Everything? No; only a few things.'

'*But* you know 'bout birds — *robins* jus' liddle robins?'

Her inflections denounced it a crime not to know. He was not proof against this, or against these.

'Oh, yes,' he said; 'of course.'

'Aha! Of course. Tha' 's what I all times thinging. Tha' 's *mis*-take by you?'

They could laugh together now.

'Ah! Tell me, then, if you please, when do those robin nest again? *Me*? I thing it is later than in Japan, is it not? Account — jus' account the robin nesting again jus' *now* in Japan.'

The consul said yes because the girl so evidently desired it — not because he knew.

'Aha! Tha' 's what I thing. Later — moach later than in Japan, is it not?'

Again her fervid emphasis obliged him to say yes, somewhat against his conscience.

'An' — sa-*ay*! When somebody gitting marry with 'nother body at your America, don' he got stay marry?'

'Usually — yes; decidedly yes; even sometimes when he doesn't wish to.'

'An' don' madder where they live?'

'Not at all.'

'Ah-h-h! *How* that is nize! Sa-*ay*; you know all 'bout *that*. What you thing?'

'Well, I know more about that than about ornithology. You see, I've been married, but I've never been a — a robin.'

The joke passed quite unnoticed. She put her great question:

'An' no one can't git divorced from 'nother *aex*cep' in a large court-house full judge?'

'Yes,' laughed the consul; 'that is true.'

'An' that take a ver' long time?'

'Yes; nearly always. The law's delay —'

'An' sometimes they git inside a jail?'

She was so avid that she risked the very great discourtesy of an interruption — and that, too, without a word of apology. Suzuki was, for an instant, ashamed for her.

'Occasionally that happens, too, I believe.'

Every doubt had been resolved in her favour.

'An' if they got a nize bebby yaet — don' they — ah, don' *aevery*body lig that?'

'I did, very much. Mine is a fine boy.'

'Sa-*ay*! He loog lig you — purple eye, bald hair, pink cheek?'

'I'm afraid he does.'

'Fraid?'

"Glad, then.'

'Oh! 'Fraid mean glad? Yaes. Tha' 's way Mr B.F. Pikkerton talking — *don'* mean what he say an' don' say what he mean — ezag'.'

The consul laughed, but he could not quite understand the drift of her questioning.

'If people have a nize bebby alig that, they don' give him away, not to no'by — *no*b'y — they don' *lig*? What you thing?'

'I should think not!' For a moment he looked savage as a young father can.

Cho-Cho-San's face glowed. She stood consciously aside, that the consul might the better see the baby on Suzuki's back. He understood, and smiled in the good-fellowship of new parenthood. He made some play with the child, and called him a fine fellow.

'Ah! You naever seen no soach bebby, I egspeg?'

In the largess of his fellowship he declared that he had not. He had only recently been engaged in putting the same question to his friends. She had hoped, indeed, that he would go on from that and say more, the subject so abundantly merited it; but she now remembered that, in her haste to satisfy her doubts, she had neglected all those innumerable little inquiries which go to make up the graceful game of Japanese courtesy. Though she might neglect them with Pinkerton, she must not with a stranger who was obliging her.

X: Gentle Lying

'Ah! How is that health? Also, I am sawry I woke you up, excellent, an' that I interrup' your languages. That is not a happy for the most exalted health — to be wake up an' interrup'. Therefore, I pray your honourable pardon. An' — how *is* that health?'

The consul said he was quite well.

'Ah, *how* that is nize! An' you always sleeping well, most honourable?'

He nodded.

'Yacs — I hear you sleep. Oh! Tha' 's not joke! No, no, no!'

He had laughed, but she would never do that.

'But I do — snore, I believe — sometimes.'

He was not proud of even this, of course.

'*Oh*! Jus' lig gen-tle bree-zes.'

He said that he could not do better than adopt this charming euphemism.

'Also, how ole you gitting ver' soon?'

'Thirty.'

A Japanese always adds a few years. She therefore thought him much younger, and her veneration abated accordingly. But he was in fact older.

'Tha' 's also nize — ver' nize. I wish I so ole. That Mr B.F. Pikkerton he lig me more if I older, I thing.' She sighed.

'I don't know about that. The American point of view differs.' But he would not meddle. 'How old are you, pray?'

This was only the proper return for her courtesy. Besides, the consul was enjoying the usually dull game of decorum to-day. The girl was piquant in a most dazzling fashion.

'Me? I 'bout — 'bout —' (what he had said made her doubt a little the Japanese idea) ''bout 'mos' twenty-seven when the chrysanthemum bloom again.'

She was seventeen.

'Yaes, 'bout 'mos' — twenty-seven —' with a barely perceptible rising inflection.

He acquiesced in the fiction, but smiled at the way she hung her head and blushed; this was not the Japanese way of telling one's age (or any other gentle lie).

'You got a grandmother?' she proceeded.

'Two,' alleged the consul.

'Tha' 's ver' splen-did. An' is she well in her healths also?'

'Which one?'

She passed the joke, if she saw it. No Japanese will make his parent the subject of one.

'The ole one — always the ole one firs'.'

The consul felt queerly chidden.

'She was well at last accounts.'

'Tha' 's nize. An' the young one?'

'The same. And now, about yours?'

'Alas! I have not that same happiness lig you. I got not ancestors whichever. They all angery account that Mr B.F. Pikkerton, so they outcast me out the family. He don' lig that they live with him, account they bag nombers. He an' me go'n' be only bag nomber, he say. He big boss bag nomber, me jus' liddle boss bag nomber. *Me*? I don' got ancestors before me nor behine me now. Hence they don' show me the way to Meido when I die. Well, me? I don' keer whichever. I got hosban' an' bebby tha' 's mos' bes' nize in Japan, mebby in the whole worl'. An' I kin go at Nirvana by 'nother road, aha! if I moast.'

Renata Scotto as Cio-Cio-San and Robert Savoie as Sharpless at Covent Garden in 1962 (photo: Zoë Dominic)

The kindly consul better than she understood both the effect of this separation of her from her 'ancestors', and the temperament of Pinkerton. He undertook, notwithstanding his resolution not to meddle, a tentative remonstrance. She listened politely, but he made no impression.

'You must not break with your relatives. If Pinkerton should not, should — well, die, you know, you would indeed be an outcast. If your own people would have nothing to do with you, nobody else would. It must, of course, be known to you that your — marriage with Pinkerton has put you in unfortunate relations with everybody; the Japanese because you have offended them, the foreigners because he has. What would you do in such a case?'

'Me? I could — dance, mebby, or — or die?'

But she laughed as she said it. Then she acknowledged his rebuking glance.

'*Aex*cuse me, tha' 's not — nize? Well, it is not so easy to die as it was — bifore he came.' She sighed happily.

The consul was curious.

'Why?' he asked.

'Why? — He make my life more sweet.'

'But that is no reason for quarrelling with your family.'

'*But* they don' wan' *me*, because my hosban' don' wan' *them*! Henceforth I got go 'way from my hosban' if I wan' them; an' if I wan' him more bedder, I got go 'way from them. No madder whichever, I got go 'way from *some* one. Well, I wan' those hosban' more bedder than any. Sa-*ay*! Tha' 's a foanny! They make me marry with him when *I* don' wish him; now I am marry with him, *they* don' wish him. Jus' after my father he kill hisself sticking with short sword, tha' 's how we gitting so poor — oh, ver' poor! Me? I go an' dance liddle, so we don' starve. Also, I thing if somebody wish me I git married for while, account that grandmother got have food an' clothings. *Well*, those ver' grandmother she as' the ole nakodo 'bout it; she lig me git marry with someone. He says man jus' as' him other day kin he git him nize wife, an' he don' know none nizer.'

She paused to let the consul make sure of this fact, which he did, and then acknowledged the appreciation she had provoked with a charming smile.

'Whichever, he say he thing I don' lig him, account he American-jin, he also remarking with me that he a barbarian an' a beas'. *Well*, me? — I say I don' wan' him. I 'fraid beas'. *But* aevery one else they say yaes — yaes, ah, yaes — he got *moaney*, an' for jus' liddle while I got endure him. So I say, "Bring me that beas'." An' lo! one day the ole nakodo he bringing him for look-at meeting. *well*! —'

She paused to laugh, and so infectious was it that the consul adventurously joined her.

'At firs' I thing him a *god*, he so tall an' beautiful, an' got on such a blue clothes all full golden things. An' he don' sit 'way, 'way off, an' jus' — *talk*!'

She laughed abandonedly.

'He make my life so ver' joyous, I thing I *nae*ver been that happy.'

She had an access of demureness.

'Oh, jus' at firs' I frighten'; account he sit so *close* with me — an' ol' my han' — an' as' if it made satin. Aha, ha, ha! Satin! Loog!'

She gave them both to him. They were deliciously pretty; but the consul was embarrassed by his possession of them. She began slowly to withdraw them, and then he let them go with regret.

'I beg your august pardon. I jus' thinging in the inside me, an' speaking with the outside. Tha' 's not nize. You don' keer nothing — 'bout — that — those?'

'What?'

He thought she meant the hands — perhaps she did.

'Jus' those — liddle — story.'

'Yes, I do,' declared the consul, with some relief; 'it is a charming story.' And it was, for Cho-Cho-San's eyes and hands took part in its telling as well as her lips.

'You mean — you lig hear more?'

'Yes.' She reflected an instant. 'I thing there is no more. Jus' — yaes, jus' after while I naever git frighten' no more — no madder how close, nor how he hol' my hand.'

'But then you — I beg pardon — you were married? I think you said so?'

'Oh, yaes,' she replied, as if that had made little difference in their situation; 'I marry with him.'

'I think his ship was then ordered to —'

She nodded.

'Alas! he got go an' serve his country. But he go'n' come back, an' keep on being marry with me. What you thing?'

The consul contrived to evade the interrogation.

'Is that why you asked about the robins?'

'Yaes; he go'n' come when the robins nest again. *He*? He don' naever egspeg we got this nize bebby, account I don' tell him. I don' kin tell him. I don' know where he is. But — *me*? I don' tell if I know, account he rush right over here, an' desert his country, an' henceforth git in a large trouble — mebby with that President United States America, an' that large Goddess Liberty Independence! What you thing?'

XI: 'The Mos' Bes' Nize Man'

It was quite superfluous to point out such of her ideas as had birth in the fertile brain of Pinkerton. Certainly he had enjoyed his married life with her, but it was for another reason than hers. The consul could observe, he thought, how exquisitely amusing it had been. It was, too, exactly in Pinkerton's line to take this dainty, vivid, eager, formless material, and mould it to his most wantonly whimisical wish. It was perhaps fortunate for her that his country had had need of him so soon after his marriage.

However, the consul informed her that her fears of trouble for Pinkerton from the sources mentioned were entirely groundless. But this, to his surprise, was not pleasing intelligence. She liked to believe (as he had let her believe) that Pinkerton occupied a large space in the affairs of his country; that he was under the special patronage of the President, and the Goddess of Liberty was, perhaps, her own corollary. But it fitted his character as she had conceived it. To her he was a god, perhaps. But let it be understood that a Japanese god is neither austere nor immaculate.

'Well, whichever,' she said, in some disappointment, 'tha' 's a so'prise on him when he come. He all times joking with me; I make one joke upon him. Tha' 's good joke. What you thing?'

The consul shook his head. The matter began to have a sinister look. But the girl's faith was sublime.

'Ah-h-h! *you*?' Her inflection was one of pity for his ignorance. 'Tha' 's account you don' know him, you shaking your nize head. He joking all times.

La Scala: Giacomo Aragall as Pinkerton (1971/72 season) and Leontyne Price as Cio-Cio-San (1960/61 season) (Archivio Fotografico Teatro alla Scala)

Sometime I dunno *if* he joking, *aex*cep' he stop, look solemn, an' laugh. *Then* he make the house raddle! Oh, mebby you thing I don' joke too, also? Well, tha' 's *mis*-take. I make joke jus' lig him — jus' bad. One time I make joke with him 'bout run 'way to that grandmother, account I don' keer for him no more. *Well* — what you thing? He say "Ello! Less see how you kin run fas'." Aha, ha, ha! Tha' 's liddle joke upon me. Now I go'n' have the larges' joke upon him. Sa-*ay* — you got tell him, if you please, augustness, that I couldn't wait, it was so long — long — long! I got tire'. So — I am marry with a great an' wise prince name' Yamadori Okyo, an' live in a huge castle with one thousan' servants, an' — an' all my hearts kin wish! Aha, ha, ha! Also, that I go'n' away to his castle with his purple-eye' bebby, to naever return no more — naever. You go'n' tell him that?'

'I would prefer not to have a hand in any further — that is, any deception,' the consul objected gravely.

The girl was amazed and reproachful.

'Ah-h-h! Don' you lig joke? I thing aevery American do. Tha' 's not nize for me. I got be sawry I telling you all those. Alas! *How* that would be nize for you! You see him git angery so quick.' She smote her hands together. 'An' then he say those remark 'bout debbil an' hell, an' rush up the hill this away.'

She again lifted her kimono, and acted it recklessly across the apartment.

'But, my dear madame —'

She came at him with a voice and movement that were resistlessly caressing. He perceived how useless it would be to protest further. He acknowledged her protean fascination.

'Ah-h-h! *Please*, augustness, to tell him? It will be that *nize* for me! Ah, you go'n' do it? — *Yaes*? Say so!'

The consul had capitulated to her voice and eyes. This was evident to her.

'Ah — thangs, most excellent. You the mos' bes' nize man in the worl' —'

She paused guiltily; even this purely Japanese euphemism might be conjugal treason.

'Except?' laughed the consul.

'*Aex*cep',' confessed the girl, with drooping head.

A smile began to grow upon her lips; when she raised her face it was a splendid laugh.

'*How* we have fun seeing him rush up that hill at the house' — she was frankly dissembling — 'so!' She illustrated again — back and forth across the apartment. 'After that — ah — after that — *well* — I make aeverything correc'.'

She was radiantly certain that she could.

The consul remembered the saying of the professor of rhetoric that no comedy could succeed without its element of tragedy. Well, Pinkerton *might* have meant to return to her. Any other man probably would. He would not have been quite certain of himself. Only, that stuff about the robins sounded like one of his infernal jokes. He probably supposed that she knew what he meant — farewell; but she had not so construed it. Unless Pinkerton had changed, he had probably not thought of her again — except as the prompt wife of another man. He never explained anything. It was his theory that circumstances always did this for one; it was therefore a saving of energy to permit circumstances to do it. There was a saying in the navy that if anyone could forget a played game or a spent bottle more quickly than Pinkerton, he had not yet been born. Providing her with a house and money meant nothing. He would probably have given her all he had, whether it were a dollar or a thousand. But, on the other hand, if she had been one of the sudden and insane fancies which occasionally visited him, the case was altogether different, and altogether like Pinkerton; for in the person of a fascinating woman the emotion might survive the absence in question. For himself, he was quite sure — had he been Pinkerton, of course — that it would have survived something greater. And finally his own views prevailed with him as if they were Pinkerton's, and he believed that he would be delighted to return and resume his charming life with her on Higashi Hill.

He thereupon told her that Lieutenant Pinkerton's ship was under orders to stop at Nagasaki, the government rendezvous for the navy, about the first of September, to observe and report the probabilities of war with China; and he was instantly glad that he had told her.

The girl's superb joy was expressed in a long, indrawn sigh, and then silence.

But something had to be said — or done.

'I — I lig as' you 'nother thing —' again dissembling, as if the talk were still at the trivialities where it began.

'Certainly,' said the consul, with a smile. 'But won't you have a chair?'

He had noticed that she was trembling. She sat up unsteadily on the edge of it. And then she forgot what she had meant to ask!

'Sa-*ay*! —' She was still at sea. But suddenly a thought flashed in her eyes.

'All bebbies at your America got those purple eye?'

'A — yes, very many of them,' said the consul, with a little surprise at her direction.

'An' — an' also bald of their head?'

'All of them, I believe, at first.'

He smiled, and the girl smiled back at him engagingly.

'Sa-*ay*, augustness, he go'n' come for see those bebby? What you thing?' Her words were like caresses.

But the rapture growing surely in the girl's face now was not reflected in that of the consul. Concern for her outweighed her fascinations for the moment.

'I — I hope so —'

She cut off his doubting incontinently.

'Sa-*ay*! Mebby you also don' thing he go'n' take us live in his large castle at United States America?' she challenged reproachfully.

'Did he tell you that he would — that he had one?'

'No; he don' tell me — *naw*thing. He laugh, when I as' him, lig the house go'n' fall down. *But* what you thing?'

The consul answered her quite briefly. He knew that he hurt her, but his impotent anger was at Pinkerton; he had not thought him capable of that.

'If I were to advise, I should ask you to consider seriously Yamadori's proposal, if he has really offered himself. It is a great and unusual opportunity for you — for any girl — in — in Japan.'

'You — thing — those —? *You*?'

She looked at him for an amazed and reproachful instant; then gathered her kimono in her hand, and pushed her feet into her clogs.

'Go before, Suzuki,' she said gently to the maid; to the consul, sorrowfully, 'Goon night.'

At the door she turned with a ceremonial sweep of her draperies, looked, and came hurrying back. All the joy had returned to her face at the sincere regret — almost pain — she saw upon his. She impulsively grasped his hands — both of them.

'Once more — different — goon night, augustness.' And her voice was very soft. 'Aha, ha, ha! *Me*? I jus' a foo-el — *yaes*. *You*? — you the mos' bes' nize man in all the whole worl' —'

She paused — smiling up at him. He understood that she wished to repeat their pretty play upon the phrase.

'Except?'

She nodded and laughed.

'*Aex*cep' — Ha, ha, ha!'

She hurried after the maid, laughing back at him confessingly as she went.

And, after all, the consul was glad it had ended thus. For joy is better than sorrow — always and everywhere.

When they again reached the pretty house on the hill, Cho-Cho-San looked ruefully back over the steep road they had come.

'Oh, *how* that was tiresome, Suzuki! But *he* — when he comes, it will be jus' — one — two — three great strides! *How* he will rush up that hill it cost us so much sweat to climb! Lig storm with lightening and thunder! Flash! flash! flash! Boum! boum! boum! An' here he is — all for jus' liddle me! Then *how* he will stamp about — not removing his boots — spoiling the mats — smashing the fusuma — shaking the house lig earthquake animal! "Where is she? Hah! Mans tole me she gone an' marry with a fool Yamadori! Gone me my purple-eye' bebby away." Then I jump roun' his neck bifore he gitting *too* angery, an' hole his han', an' say, close with his ears: "How do, Mr B.F. Pikkerton?" Aha, ha, ha! What you thing, Suzuki?'

And Suzuki said, in English, too:

'Tha' 's mos' bes' nize thing *I ae*ver see!'

XII: Like a Picture of Bunchosai

From that time until the seventeenth of September not a ship entered the harbour but under scrutiny of the glass that Lieutenant Pinkerton had left at the little house on Higashi Hill to read his signals aboard. And there were very many of them, for the war was imminent. Faith had begun to strain a little with unfaith, after the first. It was very long; but on the seventeenth his ship came into the bay. So like a great bird did she come that the glass did not find her until her white-and-gold mass veered to make an anchorage. Then, all at once, the gilt name on her bow was before Cho-Cho-San's eyes. It was tragically sudden. With a hurtling cry, she fell to the floor. The little maid, with Eastern intuition, understood; but she said nothing, and did — what was best. Both she and her mistress — and all the world, for that matter — knew the comfort of this speechless, sympathetic service. And presently she was better, and could talk.

'I — I di'n' know I *so* — glad,' softly laughed Cho-Cho-San.

But the maid had known what to expect.

'You go'n' res' liddle now, please, Oku-San! You go'n' sleep liddle — please, jus' liddle — res' — sleep?'

She drew her mistress's eyelids down, and lightly held them. Cho-Cho-San shook her off, and sprang up, revivified.

'Res'! Sleep! Not till he come!'

'Res' — peace — sleep — beauty,' chanted the maid, persuasively. But her mistress would not.

'Now, hasten lig you got eagle's wings an' a thousan' feet! It will not be one hour — not one half — till he will be here. My pink kimono — widest obi — kanzashi for my hair — an' poppies. I will be more beautiful than I have aever been. Flowers — alas! there are no cherry-blossoms. *How* that is sad! Seem lig we cannot be gay without them. In the month of the cherry-blossoms we were marry! But chrysanthemums — all of them! an' lanterns if it be black night — 'mos' one thousan'! Aha, ha, ha! His house shall be gayer than it has aever been. There shall naever again be such good occasion.'

'Res' is beauty,' urged the maid, holding up the mirror to her.

'Ah, Suzuki! I *am* beautiful — as beautiful as when he went away?'

The maid was silent — the Japanese silence which is *not* assent.

Cho-Cho-San snatched the metallic mirror out of her hand.

'I *am*!' she cried savagely. 'Say so!'

She brandished the heavy mirror over the girl's head.

'I as' you to res' — peace — sleep. Tha' 's way git beautiful once more.'

'Oh-h-h! "Once more"!' The mirror crashed to the floor, and she burst into tears.

'Jus' — you been too trouble'. Now you go'n' res' liddle,' urged the comforting maid.

'Oh, all the gods! I cannot! — I cannot till he come. I shall die bifore.'

She sorrowfully recovered the mirror.

'No — no; pitiful Kwannon, I am no longer beautiful! Waiting an' doubting make one soon sad an' old. An' how long we have wait! — how long! Oh, Shaka! But now I am happy — happier than I have aever been. Therefore shall I be more beautiful than I have aever been again. For happiness also is beauty. Ah, Suzuki, be kine with me!' She got on her knees to the maid, and laid her head at her feet. An ecstatic thought came to her. 'Suzuki, *you* shall make me beautiful today, an' to-morrow the gods shall. Now we have not even time to pray them — not time to res'. Will you not? Can you not? Ah-h-h! You *moast*!'

She pulled the girl down to her, and whispered the last words in her ear — with her arms about her.

And the girl did. Let us not inquire how. She had never yet withstood that tone and that caress. There was a certain magic in her deft fingers, and her mistress had it all. No daintier creature need one ever wish to see than this bride awaiting anew the coming of her husband.

And when it was all done, they each took a final delighted look into the mirror. It was too small to show the whole figure, but they moved it up and down and round about until every portion had been seen. They both pronounced it very good.

'Stan' jus' that way,' begged the maid, going the length of the apartment to observe. 'Jus' lig those new porcelains of Kinkozan!' she declared.

'Jus' lig those ole picture of Bunchosai!' retorted Cho-Cho-San — meaning anything but that.

But — in the way of women the world over — a few more touches were necessary — and it was finished.

'Now the flowers for his room! Take them all — oh, aevery one! We shall not need them again. Go — go — *go*! aha, ha, ha! An' Trouble — make a picture of him! He will be Trouble no longer after to-day. He go'n' git new name — mebby Joy! — Joy!'

Her commands were obeyed. Within the appointed hour the house was decked as for a festival, and not a flower remained upon its stem. The baby had indeed become a picture; and so had Cho-Cho-San and the maid and the house.

Then they hid behind the shoji, recklessly making peep-holes with their dampened fingers, as they had planned. There was one very low down for the baby, so that he could sit on the mats — which he did not choose to do — and one each for the others.

Cho-Cho-San sang as she fixed herself at her peep-hole — so as not to disarrange her finery:

'Rog-a-by, bebby, off in Japan,
You jus' a picture off of a fan.'

The maid tossed the baby like a ball into her lap.

'Aha, ha, ha!' laughed Madame Butterfly once more.

Everything was at last quite as they had planned it.

'Now let him come,' she said, in a charming defiance — 'let him come — quickly — an' — then —'

The hour passed. Then two — four. Night fell. They ceased to chatter. Later came perfect silence; then that other silence of the dead of the night. The pulses of terror quickened. Suzuki noiselessly lighted the lanterns. Later, at a shivering gesture from her mistress, she lighted the andon in their room; then the hibachi. She had grown very cold. All night they watched. He

The wait for Pinkerton: Nigi Sato (Cio-Cio-San) and Della Jones (Suzuki) at ENO, 1977 (photo: Donald Southern)

had the careless habit of the night. But he did not come.

And all the next day they watched, and many after, quite silent now, always. The baby wondered at this, and would look inquiringly from one to the other. It was very strange to him, this new silence. The house had been full always of their laughter and chatter — the patter of their feet — the sighing of the shoji. They did nothing now but watch — and eat a little, sleep a little — less and less of these. Finally Cho-Cho-San could no longer hold the glass. She lay on the mats with the baby, while the faithful handmaid watched. Every day the faded flowers were replaced by purchased ones — cheaper and cheaper ones. Their last money went for this and the candles which renewed the lights of the lanterns each night. These were not a thousand — were not a dozen — now.

She did not think of going to him. In destroying her Japanese conventions this was the one thing that had been left. In 'Onna Yushoku Mibea Bunko' ('The Young Ladies' Old Book of Decorum') she had read that the only woman who seeks a male is a yujo, a courtesan.

In a week a passenger-steamer came into the bay. They took no interest in her. But the next day, quite by accident, they saw him for the first time. He was on the deck of the strange ship. A blonde woman was on his arm. They watched quite sleeplessly all that night. A few more lanterns were lighted.

On the following morning the war-ship had disappeared from the harbour.

Cho-Cho-San was frightened. The sinking at her heart she now knew to be black doubt. Her little, unused, frivolous mind had not forecast such a catastrophe. There might have been a reason, she had conceived, for his detention aboard his ship. He was never very certain. She had not been sure that he was with her until the day before; the position of the vessel had been unfavourable for observation.

XIII: The Good Consul's Compassionate Lying

Demoralisation set in. Even the comfort of the maid was dulled. They decided that Cho-Cho-San should go and see the good consul, while the maid and the baby remained at home to welcome him if, perhaps, he had not gone with the war-ship. They had already created this hope.

The maid helped her down the steepest part of the hill. Nevertheless, when she arrived at the consulate she was quite breathless. The consul was alone. There were no frivolities now. Each knew that the other understood.

'Me? I got — liddle heart-illness, I thing,' the girl panted in excuse of her lack of ceremony and the consul's pitying stare. She looked very ill; but her smile was still tragically bright.

The consul placed her a chair. She declined it. There was a moment of conscious silence. Then he went hesitatingly to his desk, and got an envelope containing money — a large sum. He silently handed her this.

She looked at him in appealing inquiry, but she did not take the money.

'It is only — only in remembrance of the — the past. He wishes you to be always happy — as — he says he is. He confidently hopes for your good wishes and congratulations.'

There was moisture in the consul's eyes, only questioning in hers. He suddenly saw that she did not understand. He decided that she never should. He did not speak again, nor did she for a space. Then:

'Happy — happy?' she murmured dizzily. '*But* how kin *I* be happy if he do not come? How kin *he* be — happy — if — he do not come?'

The consul was silent. He still held the money toward her. She tried to smile a little, to make him think she was indifferent concerning his answer to the question she was about to ask.

'Ah — oh — *ah*! You tole him 'bout — 'bout that joke — that liddle joke we make on him?'

The consul pretended ignorance. She explained:

'That 'bout me go'n' marry with Yamadori, an' take his bebby 'way?'

He had to answer now:

'Oh, that was — too — too foolish to talk about seriously.'

Pinkerton had been glad to hear it.

'But — you — *tole* him?'

She hoped now he had not.

'Well —'

He looked out of the window. He would not strike, but she would be struck.

'But — you — you *tole* him?' She had raised her voice piteously.

'Yes,' answered the consul, dully, wondering what he could say next.

She gasped, and wiped her dry lips.

'Yaes; tha' 's — right. Tha' 's — what I — as' you do. An' — an' what he — *say*?' she questioned huskily.

The consul was willing to lie as deeply as the occasion might demand. The woe in the girl's face afflicted him. He saw in her attire the pitiful preparations to welcome the husband he now knew to be a craven, and in her face what it had cost to wait for him. But in specie the lie was difficult.

'Well,' he began uncertainly, 'we — it all happened about as you had supposed. He got very angry, and would have rushed right up the hill, as you thought, only — only —' What next? The wish to lie had grown upon him wondrously as he went on. But invention flagged. The despatches on his desk caught his eye. 'Only — he was not permitted a moment's leave while in the harbour. He had all these despatches to prepare — for — for his government — the war, you know. All in cipher.

He showed them to her. A brilliant thought came into his head.

'See! They are all in his handwriting.'

He had not written a line of them.

'His ship was ordered away suddenly to China; but he'll be back here some of these fine days, and then —'

The rest was for her. At any rate, he could lie no more.

'All — all the gods in heaven bless — you,' she said, sinking with the reaction.

She reeled, and he put her into the chair. Her head fell limply back, and her pallid face looked up at him with the weary eyes closed. But there was rest and peace on it, and it was still very beautiful.

Someone was approaching in haste, and he drew a screen before her.

XIV: The Blonde Woman

A woman entered.

'Mr Sharpless — the American consul?' she asked, while crossing the threshold.

The consul bowed.

'Can you reach my husband at Kobe — by telegraph?'

'I think so. Who is your husband?'

He took up a writing-pad as he spoke.

'Lieutenant Pinkerton of the —.'

'One moment, for God's sake!'

It was too late. The eyes of the little woman in the chair were fixed on his. They even tried to smile a little, wearily, at the poor result of his compassionate lying. She shook her head for silence.

'I beg your pardon; I'm — I am — ready —' said the consul, roughly. He made no other explanation. 'Proceed.'

'I should like you to send this telegram: "Just saw the baby and his nurse. Can't we have him at once? He is lovely. Shall see the mother about it to-morrow. Was not at home when I was there to-day. Expect tomorrow. Was not at home when I was there to-day. Expect to join you Wednesday week per *Kioto Maru*. May I bring him along? Adelaide."'

As she advanced and saw Cho-Cho-San, she stopped in open admiration.

'How very charming — how *lovely* — you are, dear! Will you kiss me, you pretty — *plaything*!'

Cho-Cho-San stared at her with round eyes — as children do when afraid. Then her nostrils quivered and her lids slowly closed.

'No,' she said, very softly.

'Ah, well,' laughed the other, 'I don't blame you. They say you don't do that sort of thing — to women, at any rate. I quite forgive our men for falling in love with you. Thanks for permitting me to interrupt you. And, Mr Sharpless, will you get that off at once? Good day!'

She went with the hurry in which she had come. It was the blonde woman they had seen on the deck of the passenger-steamer.

They were quite silent after she was gone — the consul still at his desk, his head bowed impotently in his hands.

Cho-Cho-San rose presently, and staggered toward him. She tried desperately to smile, but her lips were tightly drawn against her teeth. Searching unsteadily in her sleeve, she drew out a few small coins, and held them out to him. He curiously took them on his palm.

'They are his, all that is left of his beautiful moaney. I shall need no more. Give them to him. I lig if you also say I sawry — no, no, *no*! glad — glad — *glad*!' She humbly sighed. '*Me*? I — I wish him that happiness same lig he wish for himself — an' — an' — me. *Me*? I shall — be happy — mebby. Tell him I — shall be — happy.'

Her head drooped for a moment. When she raised it she was quite emotionless, if one might judge from her face.

'Thang him — that Mr B.F. Pikkerton — also for all that kineness he have been unto me. Permit me to thang *you*, augustness, for that same. You — you' — she could smile a little now at the pretty recollection — then the tears came slowly into her eyes — 'You — the mos' bes' nize man — in all the — whole — worl'.'

She closed her eyes a moment, and stood quite still.

The consul said below his breath:

'— Pinkerton, and all such as he!'

'Goon night,' said Cho-Cho-San, and at the door looking back, 'Sayonara,' and another tired smile.

She staggered a little as she went out.

'Alas, you also have seen her!' wailed the intuitive little maid, as she let her mistress in.

Yasuko Hayashi as Cio-Cio-San at Covent Garden in 1978 (photo: Donald Southern)

'An' she is more beautiful than the Sun-Goddess,' answered Cho-Cho-San.

The maid knelt to take off her shoes.

'She — she thing me — jus' a — plaything.'

She generously tried to smile at the maid, who was weeping. She touched her hair caressingly as she knelt.

'Don' weep for me, liddle maiden — account I disappoint — a liddle — disappoint — Don' weep for me. That liddle while ago you as' me to res' — peace — sleep,' she said after a while, wearily. 'Well, go 'way, an' I will — res'. Now I *wish* to res' — sleep. Long — long sleep. An' I pray you, loog, when you see me again, whether I be not again beautiful — again as a bride.'

The maid did not go. Once more she understood her mistress.

'*But* I thing *you* loave me?'

The girl sobbed.

'Therefore go — that I suffer no more. Go, that I res' — peace — sleep. Long — beautiful sleep! Go, I beg.'

She gently took her hands and led her out.

'Farewell, liddle maiden,' she said softly, closing the shoji. 'Don' weep.'

She sat quite still, and waited till night fell. Then she lighted the andon, and drew her toilet-glass toward her. She had a sword in her lap as she sat down. It was the one thing of her father's which her relatives had permitted her to keep. It would have been very beautiful to a Japanese, to whom the sword is a soul. A golden dragon writhed about the superb scabbard. He had eyes of rubies, and held in his mouth a sphere of crystal which meant many mystical things to a Japanese. The guard was a coiled serpent of exquisite workmanship. The blade was tempered into vague shapes of beasts at the edge. It was signed, 'Ikesada'. To her father it had been Honour. On the blade was this inscription:

To die with Honour
When one can no longer live with Honour.

It was in obscure ideographs; but it was also written on her father's kaimyo at the shrine, and she knew it well.

'To die with honour —' She drew the blade affectionately across her palm. Then she made herself pretty with vermilion and powder and perfumes; and she prayed, humbly endeavouring at the last to make her peace. She had not forgotten the missionary's religion; but on the dark road from death to Meido it seemed best now to trust herself to the compassionate augustnesses, who had always been true.

Then she placed the point of the weapon at that nearly nerveless spot in the neck known to every Japanese, and began to press it slowly inward. She could not help a little gasp at the first incision. But presently she could feel the blood finding its way down her neck. It divided on her shoulder, the larger stream going down her bosom. In a moment she could see it making its way daintily between her breasts. It began to congeal there. She pressed on the sword, and a fresh stream swiftly overran the other — redder, she thought. And then suddenly she could no longer see it. She drew the mirror closer. Her hand was heavy, and the mirror seemed far away. She knew that she must hasten. But even as she locked her fingers on the serpent of the guard, something within her cried out piteously. They had taught her how to die, but he had taught her how to live — nay, to make life sweet. Yet that was the reason she must die. Strange reason! She now first knew that it was sad to die. He had come, and substituted himself for everything; he had gone, and left her nothing — nothing but this.

The maid softly put the baby into the room. She pinched him, and he began to cry.

'Oh, pitiful Kwannon! Nothing?'

The sword fell dully to the floor. The stream between her breasts darkened and stopped. Her head drooped slowly forward. Her arms penitently outstretched themselves toward the shrine. She wept.

'Oh pitiful Kwannon!' she prayed.

The baby crept cooing into her lap. The little maid came in and bound up the wound.

When Mrs Pinkerton called next day at the little house on Higashi Hill it was quite empty.

Thematic Guide

Many of the themes from the opera have been identified in the articles by numbers in square brackets, which refer to the themes set out on these pages. The themes are also identified by the numbers in square brackets at the corresponding points in the libretto, so that the words can be related to the musical themes.

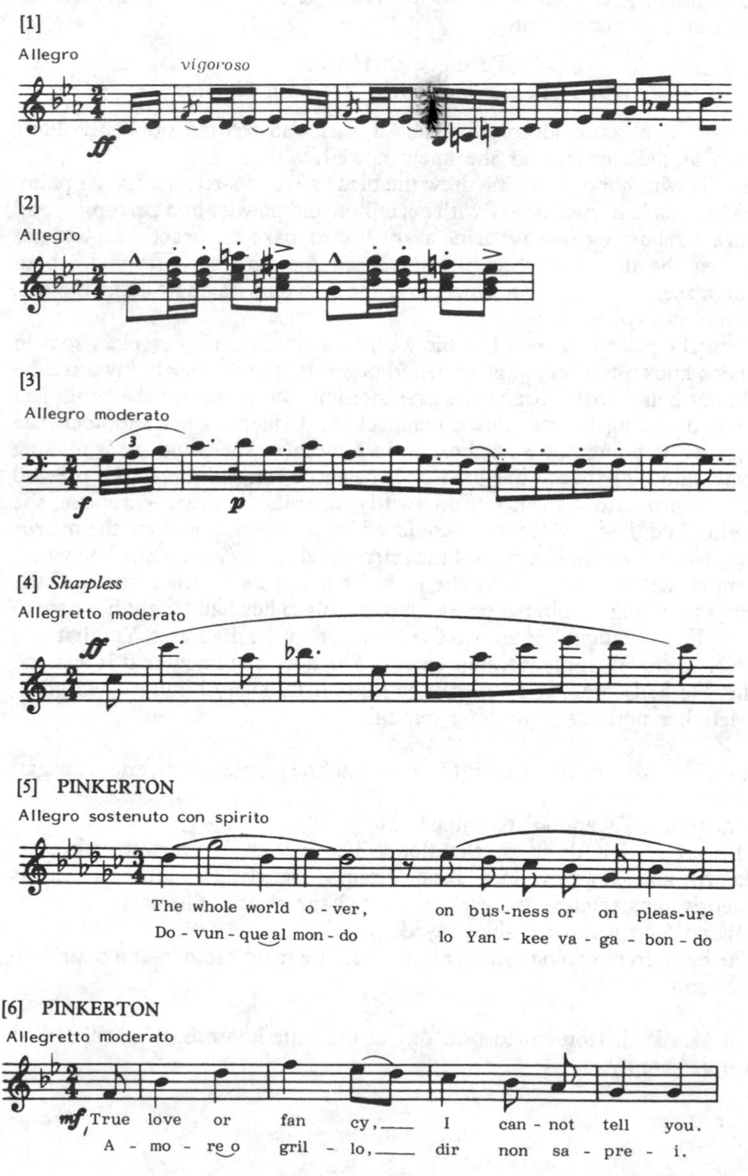

[7] SHARPLESS

[8a]

[8b]

[9]

Largo

ppp

[10]

[11] BUTTERFLY

[12]

[13] **SHARPLESS** **PINKERTON**

Moderato

[14] **WEDDING CHORUS**

Allegro molto moderato, mollemente

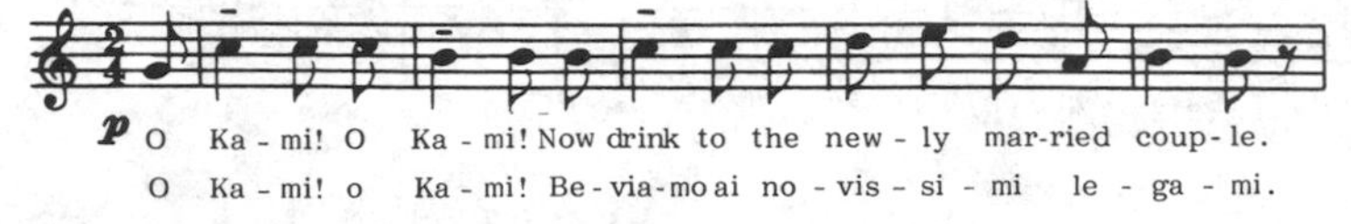

[15] *The Curse*

Allegro moderato

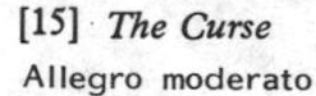

[16] **PINKERTON**

Andantino calmo

[17] **PINKERTON**

Andante lento

[18] **BUTTERFLY**

Andante sostenuto

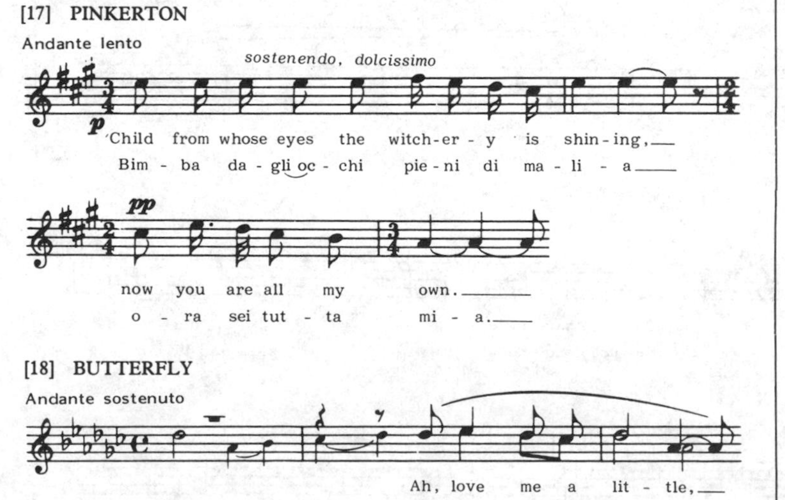

[19] **BUTTERFLY**

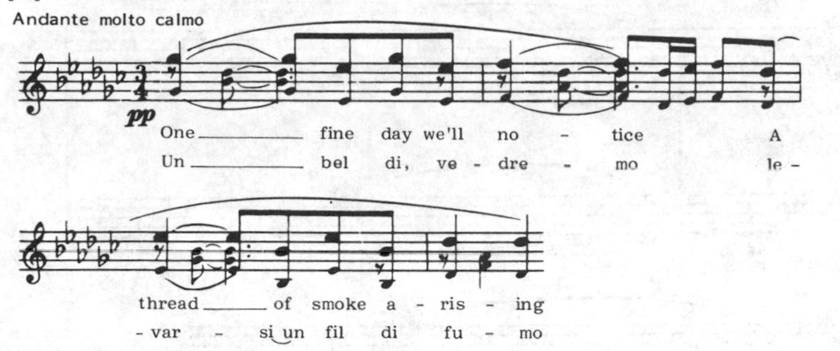

[20] **BUTTERFLY**

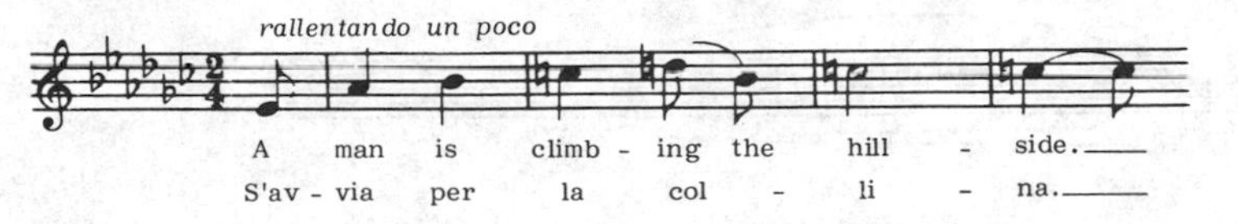

[21]

Allegro

ff

[22] **BUTTERFLY**

[23]

[24]

Andantino mosso

[25]

Allegro moderato

[26] **BUTTERFLY**

Andante molto mosso

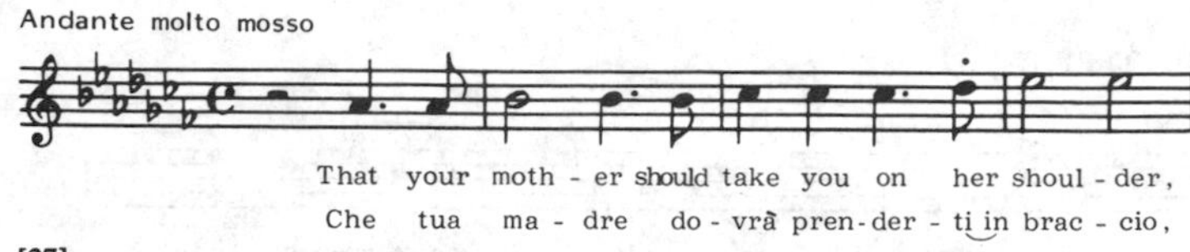

[27]

Andante

[28] **BUTTERFLY** / *Flower Duet*

Andantino mosso

[29]

Allegretto moderato

[30] BUTTERFLY
Allegretto mosso
Ah, but the balm - y breath of spring shall breathe
Tut - ta la pri - ma - ve - ra vo - glio
[31] BUTTERFLY
Allegretto moderato
Balm - y breath of spring shall breathe her sweet - ness here.
Tutta - la pri - ma - ve - ra vo - glio che o - lez - zi qui.
[32] BUTTERFLY, SUZUKI
Allegro molto moderato
a tempo ma sempre un po sostenendo
ten. sostenendo
In hand - fuls let us scat - ter vi - o - lets and mi - mo - sa
Get - tia - mo a ma - ni pie - ne mam-mo - le e tu - be - ro - se,
[33]
Andante sostenuto
espress.
[34]
Moderato
[35]
Largo
[36] PINKERTON
Andante lento
Fare - well, oh hap - py home! Fare - well, home of love!
Ad - di - o, fio - ri - to a - sil di le - ti - zia e d'a - mor!
[37] BUTTERFLY
Andante sostenuto
My son, sent down from Heav - en, from Pa - ra - dise des - cen - ded
O a me, sce - so dal tro - no del - l'al - to Pa - ra - di - so,

Elisabeth Rethberg as Cio-Cio-San. Toscanini called her the perfect soprano and she sang the title role at Covent Garden in 1925.

Madam Butterfly
Madama Butterfly
A Japanese Tragedy

An Opera in Two Acts by Giacomo Puccini

Libretto by Giuseppe Giacosa and Luigi Illica
after the book by John Luther Long
and the play by David Belasco

English version based on that of R.H. Elkin

Madam Butterfly was first performed at the Teatro alla Scala, Milan on February 17, 1904 for one night only. A revised three-act version was first seen at Brescia on May 28, 1904. After more revisions, the now traditional version was established for performances at the Opéra Comique, Paris on December 28, 1906. The first performance in England was at Covent Garden on July 10, 1905. The first performance in the United States was in Washington on October 15, 1906.

This Italian libretto is the one performed at the 1904 première at La Scala. The footnotes give the texts of the passages which Puccini altered, and details of when he did so. The full text of the 1906 version, which has become traditional, can only therefore be found by reading the notes as well. R.H. Elkin's English translation was made for the American performances in October 1906 and so includes some passages which Puccini altered for Paris. On the other hand it does not cover quite all the original text and I have supplied literal translations which are marked in square brackets, for the gaps. Many changes have been made to R.H. Elkin's translation over the years: this text reflects what is currently performed by ENO. — Ed.

CHARACTERS

Madam Butterfly, Cho-Cho-San (Madama Butterfly, Cio-Cio-San)	*soprano*
Suzuki *her servant*	*mezzo-soprano*
Kate Pinkerton	*mezzo-soprano*
F.B. Pinkerton* *Lieutenant in the U.S. Navy*	*tenor*
Sharpless *U.S. Consul in Nagasaki*	*baritone*
Goro *a marriage broker*	*tenor*
Prince Yamadori	*baritone*
The Bonze *Butterfly's uncle*	*bass*
The Imperial Commissioner	*bass*
The Official Registrar	*baritone*
Butterfly's Mother	*mezzo-soprano*
The Aunt	*mezzo-soprano*
The Cousin	*soprano*
Sorrow (Dolor) *Butterfly's child*	—
Butterfly's Relatives and Friends, Servants	

Time: the present (i.e. 1904)
Place: A hill near Nagasaki

* Pinkerton's original Christian names were changed in the 1904 libretto presumably because the librettists thought that English-speaking audiences would take B.F. to stand for 'bloody fool' rather than 'Benjamin Franklin'. 'Sir Francis Blummy' was, however, short-lived because R.H. Elkin reverted to the original John Luther Long names in his translation, and the traditional 1906 Paris version also reverts to them.

Yoko Watanabe as Cio-Cio-San at Covent Garden in 1983 (photo: Donald Southern)

Act One

A Japanese house, terrace and garden. Below, in the background, is the bay, harbour and town of Nagasaki. From the room at the back of the little house, Goro, with much bowing, leads in Pinkerton; with much ostentation but still obsequiously he draws his attention to the details of the structure. Goro makes a partition slide out at the back, and explains its use to Pinkerton. They come forward a little onto the terrace. [1, 2]

PINKERTON
(*surprised at all he sees*)

So the walls and the ceiling . . .

E soffitto . . . e pareti . . .

GORO
(*enjoying Pinkerton's surprise*)

Come and go at your pleasure
However you may fancy.
Every room, every doorway —
As you see it is really most convenient.

Vanno e vengono a prova
a norma che vi giova
nello stesso locale
alternar nuovi aspetti ai consueti.

PINKERTON
(*looking around*)

And can you tell me, where's
The bedroom?

Il nido nuziale
dov'è?

GORO
(*pointing in two directions*)

Here or there! . . . depending . . .

Qui, o là! . . . secondo . . .

PINKERTON

A wonderful contrivance!
The hallway?

Anch'esso a doppio fondo!
La sala?

GORO
(*showing the terrace*)

Here, sir.

Ecco!

PINKERTON
(*amazed*)

In the open? . . .

All'aperto? . . .

GORO
(*making the partitions slide out*)

The wall slides outward . . .

Un fianco scorre . . .

PINKERTON
(*while Goro is making the partitions slide out*)

I see now! . . . Another . . .

Capisco! Un altro . . .

GORO

Slides along!

Scivola!

PINKERTON

But is the whole thing strong enough?

E la dimora frivola . . .

GORO
(*protesting*)

Strong as a marriage contract,
Secure from floor to ceiling.

Salda come una torre
da terra, infino al tetto . . .

(*He invites Pinkerton to go down the garden.*)

PINKERTON

And it works just as smoothly.

È una casa a soffietto.

GORO

(*He claps his hands loudly three times. Two men and a woman enter. They humbly and slowly go down on their knees before Pinkerton.*)

This is the trusty handmaid	Questa è la cameriera
Who'll wait upon your wife,	che della vostra sposa
Faithful and devoted.	fu già serva amorosa.
The houseboy . . . And this the cook. They're embarrassed	Il cuoco . . . il servitor. Sono confusi
At such great honour.	del grande onore.

PINKERTON
(*impatiently*)

Their names?	I nomi?

GORO
(*pointing to Suzuki*)

Miss Gentle Breeze of Morning.	Miss Nuvola leggiera. —
(*pointing to one servant and then the other*)	
Ray of the Golden Sunbeam. Sweet-scented Pinetree.	Raggio di sol nascente. — Esala aromi.

PINKERTON

Foolishly chosen nicknames! *1	Nomi di scherno o scherzo.
I will call them scarecrows!	Io li chiamerò: musi!
(*pointing to them one by one*)	
Scarecrow first, scarecrow second, and scarecrow third!	Muso primo, secondo, e muso terzo.

[1]

SUZUKI
(*still on her knees, growing bolder, raises her head*)

I think Your Honour is smiling.	Sorride Vostro Onore? —
A smile is like a flower,	Il riso è frutto e fiore.
Said the wise Ocunama:	Disse il savio Ocunama:
A smile conquers all, and	dei crucci la trama
Defies every trouble. Pearls may be won by smiling;	smaglia il sorriso. Schiude alla perla il guscio,
Smiles can even open	apre all'uom l'uscio
The gates of Heaven.	del Paradiso.
The perfume of the Gods,	Profumo degli Dei . . .
The fountain of Life . . .	Fontana della vita . . .

(*Goro perceives that Pinkerton begins to be bored by Suzuki's loquacity. He claps his hands three times. The three rise and quickly disappear into the house.*) [1]

PINKERTON

When women start to talk,	A chiacchiere costei
I find them all the same.	mi par cosmopolita.
(*to Goro who has gone to the back to look out*)	
What is it?	Che guardi?

GORO

I am watching for the bride.	Se non giunge ancor la sposa.

PINKERTON

Are we ready?	Tutto è pronto?

GORO

Every detail.	Ogni cosa.

(*He bows ingratiatingly.*)

PINKERTON

A most efficient fellow.	Gran perla di sensale!

---

*1 This speech was cut for the 1906 Paris version.

GORO

There will come: the official
Registrar, the relations, and then your Consul,
Your future wife. Then you'll sign the contract
And solemnize the marriage.

[3] Qui verran: l'Ufficiale
del registro, i parenti, il vostro Console,
la fidanzata. Qui si firma l'atto
e il matrimonio è fatto.

PINKERTON

Are there many relations?

E son molti i parenti?

GORO

Her mother, grandma, and the Bonze, her uncle,
(Who'll hardly honour us with his appearance)
And her cousins, male and female,
With ancestors, I reckon . . .
And other blood relations, a round two dozen.
As to your descendants . . .

La suocera, la nonna, lo zio Bonzo
(che non ci degnerà di sua presenza)
e cugini! e le cugine . . .
Mettiam fra gli ascendenti
ed i collaterali, un due dozzine.
Quanto alla discendenza . . .

(*with obsequious presumption*)

That matter can be safely
Left to you, sir, and lovely Butterfly.

provvederanno assai
Vostra Grazia e la bella Butterfly.

PINKERTON

A most efficient fellow!

Gran perla di sensale!

(*Goro thanks him with a deep bow.*)

SHARPLESS
(*off-stage, quite distant*)

It can't be much further now!
Stumbling! And spluttering!

E suda e arrampica!
e sbuffa e inciampica!

GORO
(*who has run to the background, announces:*)

Here comes the Consul.

[4] Il Consol sale.

SHARPLESS
(*He enters, quite out of breath. Goro bows low before the Consul.*)

Ah! The climb up here
Has left me breathless!

Ah! . . . quei ciottoli
M'hanno sfiaccato!

PINKERTON
(*He goes to meet the Consul: they shake hands.*)

You're very welcome.

Bene arrivato.

SHARPLESS

Ough!

Ouff!

PINKERTON

Quickly, Goro,
Fetch some refreshment.

Presto, Goro,
qualche ristoro.

(*Goro hurries into the house.*)

SHARPLESS
(*panting and looking around*)

It's high here.

Alto.

PINKERTON
(*pointing to the view*)

But lovely!

Ma bello!

SHARPLESS

(*looking at the sea and the town below*)

Nagasaki, the ocean,
The harbour . . .

Nagasaki, il mare!
il porto . . .

PINKERTON

(*pointing to the house*)

This house is so fragile
That it stands up by magic.

E una casetta
che obbedisce a bacchetta.

SHARPLESS

Yours?

Vostra?

PINKERTON

Yes I have bought
It for nine hundred and ninety-nine years,
But with the option, at every
Month, to cancel the contract!
I must say, in this country,
The houses and the contracts are elastic!

La comperai
per novecento novantanove anni,
con facoltà, ogni mese,
di rescindere i patti.
Sono in questo paese
elastici del par, case e contratti.

SHARPLESS

So easy if you have no conscience.

E l'uomo esperto ne profitta.

(*Goro comes bustling out of the house, followed by the two servants. They bring glasses and bottles and two wicker chairs; placing the glasses and bottles on a small table, they return to the house.*)

PINKERTON

(*inviting Sharpless to be seated*)

Surely.

Certo.

(*frankly*)

The whole world over, on business or on pleasure, [5]
the Yankee travels
and scorns all danger.
He casts his anchor wherever he chooses . . .

Dovunque al mondo lo yankee vagabondo
si gode e traffica
sprezzando i rischi.
Affonda l'ancora alla ventura . . .

(*He breaks off to offer Sharpless a drink.*)

You'll have a whisky?

Milk-punch, o Wisky?

(*resuming*)

. . . till with a change of wind
the ship swings round, then up go sails and rigging.
And life is not worth living
If he can't win the fairest
Pearl of every country . . .
And then fire her with love.

. . . finchè una raffica
scompigli nave, ormeggi, alberatura.
La vita ei non appaga
se non fa suo tesor
i fiori d'ogni plaga,
d'ogni bella gli amor.

SHARPLESS

A very easy gospel
Which makes life very pleasant,
But is fatal in the end.

È un facile vangelo
che fa la vita vaga
ma che intristisce il cuor.

PINKERTON

(*continuing*)

Fate cannot crush him, he tries again undaunted.
No-one and nothing
Can break his spirit.
And so I'm marrying in Japanese style
For the next nine
Hundred and ninety-nine
Years. Free, though, to annul the marriage monthly!

Vinto si tuffa e la sorte riacciuffa
Il suo talento
fa in ogni dove.
Così mi sposo all'uso giapponese
per novecento
novantanove
anni. Salvo a prosciogliermi ogni mese.

(*standing up and raising his glass to Sharpless*)

'America for ever!'

'America for ever!'

SHARPLESS

'America for ever!'

'America for ever'

(They sit down on the terrace again.)

— Is the bride
Very pretty?

— Ed è bella
la sposa?

GORO

(having overheard, approaches the terrace, eagerly and officiously)

Fair as a garland
Of fragrant flowers. Brighter than a
Star in the heavens.
And so cheap too; one hundred
Yen!

Una ghirlanda
di fiori freschi. Una stella
dai raggi d'oro.
E per nulla: sol cento
yen.

(to the Consul)

And if Your Honour would command me,
I have a fine selection ...

Se Vostra Grazia mi comanda
ce n'ho un assortimento.

(The Consul laughingly declines.)

PINKERTON

(very impatiently)

Go and meet her, Goro.

Va, conducila Goro.

(Goro runs to the back and disappears down the hill.)

SHARPLESS

Are you out of your senses,
Or is this some
infatuation?

Quale smania vi prende!
Sareste addirittura
cotto?

PINKERTON

(rising impatiently; Sharpless rises also)

Perhaps, who knows? Depends what
You call infatuation!

Non so! non so! Dipende
dal grado di cottura!

True love or fancy,
I cannot tell you. All that I know is,
She, with her innocent charm, has
entranced me.

[6] Amore o grillo,
dir non saprei. — Certo costei
m'ha colle ingenue — arti invescato.

Almost transparently fragile and slender,
Dainty in stature, quaint little figure,
She seems to have stepped down straight
from a screen.

Lieve qual tenue — vetro soffiato
alla statura — al portamento
sembra figura — da paravento.

But from her background of varnish and
lacquer,
Suddenly light as a feather she flutters,
A butterfly that is hovering and settling,
Silently charming and yet so seductive.
I'm all afire for her ... I must pursue her ...
Although her wings might, in the game, be
broken.

Ma dal suo lucido — fondo di lacca
come con subito — moto si stacca,
qual farfalletta — svolazza e posa
con tal grazietta — silenziosa
che di rincorrerla — furor m'assale
se pure infrangerne — dovessi l'ale.

SHARPLESS

(seriously and kindly)

The other day, she came to
The Consulate all alone.
I did not see her, but I heard her speak.
And the mystery of her
Voice touched my very soul.
Surely, love that is pure
And true speaks like that.
It would indeed be a pity
To tear those delicate wings,
And far too cruel to torment a trusting
heart.
No cry of anguish

[7] Ier l'altro, il Consolato
Sen' venne a visitar!
Io non la vidi, ma l'udii parlar.
Di sua voce il mistero
l'anima mi colpì.
Certo quando è sincer
l'amor parla così.
Sarebbe gran peccato
le lievi ali strappar
e desolar forse un credulo cuor.
Quella — divina

Should ever be uttered.	mite — vocina
By that gentle and trusting little voice.	non dovrebbe dar note di dolor.

PINKERTON

Dearly beloved Consul,	Console mio garbato,
You know I mean no harm!	quetatevi! Si sa,
Men of your age look on life with mournful eyes.	la vostra età è di flebile umor.
No harm I reckon	Non c'è gran male
To play this game	s'io vo' quell'ale
And guide her to the tender flights of love!	drizzar ai dolci voli dell'amor!

(He offers him more to drink.)

Whisky?	Wisky?

SHARPLESS

Yes, give me another.	Un altro bicchiere.

(Pinkerton mixes Sharpless some whisky and also fills up his own glass. Sharpless raises his glass.)

Here's to your friends and relations at home.	Bevo alla vostra famiglia lontana.

PINKERTON
(raises his glass)

And here's to my real wedding day when I will	E al giorno in cui mi sposerò con vere
Marry a real wife from America.	nozze, a una vera sposa . . . americana.

GORO
(reappears, running breathlessly up the hill)

See them! They've mounted the summit of the hill!	Ecco! Son giunte al sommo del pendio.

(pointing towards the path)

A crowd of women hustling,	Già del femmineo sciame
Like the wind in branches rustling,	qual di vento in fogliame
Here they come bustling!	s'ode il brusio.

(Pinkerton and Sharpless retire to the back of the garden, and look out at the path on the hillside.)

BUTTERFLY'S GIRL-FRIENDS
(off-stage)

Ah! Ah! What a sea, and what a sky!	[8a, 9]	Ah! Ah! Quanto cielo! quanto mar!

BUTTERFLY
(off-stage)

Just one more step to climb.	Ancora un passo or via.

THE GIRL-FRIENDS

How long you tarry.	Come sei tarda.
At last the summit.	Ecco la vetta.
Look, oh look, the mass of flowers!	Guarda, guarda, quanti fior!

BUTTERFLY
(still off-stage; serenely)

One moment.		Aspetta.
Across the earth and o'er the ocean,		Spira sul mare e sulla
Balmy breeze and scent of spring are blowing —		terra un primaveril soffio giocondo.
I am the happiest maiden,		Io sono la fanciulla
The happiest in Japan. Yes, I am happy,		più lieta del Giappone, anzi del mondo.
For I've obeyed the summons,		Amiche, io son venuta
The sweet summons of love,	[10]	al richiamo d'amor. . .
Upon the threshold standing —		venni alle soglie
Ah, here the glory		ove s'accoglie
That life or death can offer doth now await me.		il bene di chi vive e di chi muor.

THE GIRL-FRIENDS

Best of luck, good luck attend you,	Gioia a te, gioia a te sia
Gentle maiden, but ere	dolce amica, ma pria
You go beyond the threshold which invites you,	di varcar la soglia che ti attira
Turn and admire	volgiti e mira
The things you hold the dearest!	le cose tutte che ti son si care.
The lovely flowers, the lovely sky and the sea!	Quanto cielo! Quanti fiori! Quanto mar!

SHARPLESS

Oh, happy prattle, careless days of youth!	O allegro cinguettar di gioventù!

(*Butterfly and her girl-friends appear on stage. They all carry large brightly-coloured, open sunshades.*)

BUTTERFLY
(*to her friends*)

We're there now.	Siam giunte.

(*She sees the three men standing together and recognizes Pinkerton. She quickly closes her sunshade and at once introduces him to her friends.*)

F.B. Pinkerton. Down.	F.B. Pinkerton. Giù.

(*She goes down on her knees.*)

THE GIRL-FRIENDS
(*closing their sunshades and going down on their knees*)

Down.	Giù.

(*They all rise and ceremoniously approach Pinkerton.*)

BUTTERFLY

We are honoured.	Gran ventura.

THE GIRL-FRIENDS
(*bowing*)

We are honoured.	Riverenza.

PINKERTON
(*smiling*)

Did you find it	È un po' dura
Rather tiring?	la scalata?

BUTTERFLY
(*in a measured way*)

To a bride it's	A una sposa
Not as tiring	costumata
As the weary	più penosa
Hours of waiting . . .	l'impazienza.

PINKERTON
(*kindly, but a little teasingly*)

What a compliment	Molto raro
To me.	complimento.

BUTTERFLY
(*ingenuously*)

I know better	Dei più belli
Things than that . . .	ancor ne so.

PINKERTON

Yes, I'm certain.	Dei gioielli!

BUTTERFLY
(*anxious to show off her stock of compliments*)

I could tell you	Se vi è caro
Some this moment . . .	sul momento . . .

PINKERTON

Thank you . . . no.	Grazie — no.

SHARPLESS

(*After scanning the group of maidens with curiosity, he approaches Butterfly who listens to him attentively.*)

Miss 'Butterfly'. How pretty, your name was well chosen. Are you from Nagasaki?	Miss 'Butterfly'. Bel nome che vi sta a meraviglia. Siete di Nagasaki?

BUTTERFLY

Yes I am, sir. My people Were formerly wealthy.	Signor si. Di famiglia assai prospera un tempo.

(*to her friends*)

That is so!	Verità?

THE GIRL-FRIENDS

(*assenting with alacrity*)

That is so!	Verità!

BUTTERFLY

(*quite naturally*)

For no-one likes to own that he in poverty was born. Is not every beggar, when you listen to his tale, Of ancient lineage? And yet Indeed I have known riches. But the strongest oak must fall When the storm uproots the forest . . . and we had to go as geisha To earn our living.	Nessuno si confessa mai nato in povertà, e non c'è vagabondo che a sentirlo non sia di gran prosapia. Eppure senza millanteria conobbi la ricchezza. Ma il turbine rovescia le quercie più robuste — e abbiam fatto la ghescia per sostentarci.

(*to her friends*)

Truly!	Vero?

THE GIRL-FRIENDS

(*corroborating*)

Truly!	Vero!

BUTTERFLY

I don't deny it, And don't blush for it.	Non lo nascondo, nè mi adonto.

(*noticing that Sharpless smiles*)

You're laughing? But why? . . . That's how the world runs.	Ridete? Perchè? . . . Cose del mondo.

PINKERTON

(*He has listened with interest and turns to Sharpless.*)

(With her youthful innocence she sets my heart throbbing . . .)	(Con quel fare di bambola quando parla m'infiamma.)

SHARPLESS

(*He, too, is interested in Butterfly's prattle and continues to question her.*)

And have you no sisters?	E ci avete sorelle?

BUTTERFLY

No, Your Honour. There's my mother.	No signore. Ho la mamma.

GORO

(*importantly*)

A most dignified lady.	Una nobile dama.

BUTTERFLY

But through no fault whatever, She is now very poor.	Ma senza farle torto povera molto anch'essa.

SHARPLESS

And your father?	E vostro padre?

BUTTERFLY
(stops short in surprise then answers very briefly)

Dead. [12]	Morto.

*(The friends hang their heads. Goro is embarrassed. They all fan themselves nervously. To break the painful silence, Butterfly turns to Pinkerton.)**2

But I have other relations: There is the Bonze, my uncle.	Ma ho degli altri parenti: uno zio Bonzo.

PINKERTON
(with exaggerated surprise)

Never!	Senti!

THE GIRL-FRIENDS

A miracle of wisdom!	Un mostro di sapienza!

GORO
(warmly)

Of eloquence a fountain!	Un fiume d'eloquenza!

PINKERTON

Thank you, thank you, kind Fate!	Grazie, grazie, mio Dio!

BUTTERFLY

And yet another uncle! But that one . . .	Ci ho pure un altro zio! Ma quello . . .

THE GIRL-FRIENDS

Good for nothing!	Gran corbello!

BUTTERFLY
(kind-heartedly trying to hush them up)

. . . is just a little wanting.	. . . ha un po' la testa a zonzo.

THE GIRL-FRIENDS

An everlasting tippler.	Perpetuo tavernaio.

PINKERTON

One thinker, and one drinker! They make a pretty couple.	Capisco — un Bonzo e un gonzo. — I due mi fanno il paio.

BUTTERFLY
(mortified)

You are not angry?	Ve ne rincresce?

PINKERTON

Not I! I do not care a jot! *	Ohibò! Per quel che me ne fo!

SHARPLESS
(returning to Butterfly)

May I ask your age?	Quanti anni avete?

BUTTERFLY
(with almost childish coquetry)

Now try to guess it!	Indovinate.

PINKERTON

Ten years.	Dieci.

*2 The following discussion of the Uncles, up to the asterisk, was cut from the 1906 Paris version.

BUTTERFLY

Guess higher. | Crescete.

SHARPLESS

Twenty. | Venti.

BUTTERFLY

Guess lower. | Calate.
Come let me whisper softly. | Quindici netti, netti;
(*slyly*)
I am old, am I not? | sono vecchia diggià.

SHARPLESS

Did you know that? | Quindici anni!

PINKERTON

Yes, I knew it. | Quindici anni.

SHARPLESS

The age | L'età
For dolls and . . . | dei giuochi . . .

PINKERTON

. . . and getting married! | . . . e dei confetti.

(*To Goro, who claps his hands to summon the three servants who come running out of the house.*)

Call my scarecrows to hand round *3 | Qua i tre musi. Servite
Candied flies and spiders, | ragni e mosche candite.
Preserves and pastry and all sorts | Nidi al giulebbe e quale
Of curious liquors, | è licor più indigesto
And most peculiar delicacies that | e più nauseabonda leccornia
They fancy in Japan. | della Nipponeria.

(*Goro signals to the servants to hurry into the house to bring out everything. Having received fresh orders from Pinkerton, Goro is just going into the house himself when he perceives some more people climbing the hill; he goes to look, then runs to announce the new arrivals to Pinkerton and Sharpless.*)

GORO
(*announcing with importance*)

The august High Commissioner, the official | L'Imperial Commissario e l'Ufficiale
Registrar, the relations. | del registro — i congiunti.

PINKERTON
(*to Goro*)

Come now, hurry. | Fate presto.

(*Goro runs into the house. In the background Butterfly's relations are seen climbing the hill and passing along the path; Butterfly and her friends go to meet them, bowing and kow-towing; the relations stare curiously at the two Americans. Pinkerton has taken Sharpless by the arm and, leading him to one side, laughingly makes him look at the quaint group of relations.*)

PINKERTON

Truly comic this procession, | Che burletta la sfilata
Meet my worthy new relations | della nova parentela
Held on terms of monthly contract! | tolta in prestito, a mesata.

I feel sure that there, behind the | Certo dietro a quella vela
Mighty fan of peacock's feathers, | di ventaglio pavonazzo,
My mother-in-law is hiding. | la mia suocera si cela.

(*pointing to Yakusidé*)

And that shabby-looking ninny | E quel coso da strapazzo
Is the mad and boozy uncle. | è lo zio briaco e pazzo.

---

*3 This speech was cut in the 1906 Paris version.

RELATIONS AND FRIENDS
(*to Butterfly*)

Where is he? Where is he? | Dov'è? dove'è?

BUTTERFLY AND OTHER FRIENDS
(*pointing to Pinkerton*)

Look, there he is. | Eccolo là!

FIRST COUSIN AND SOME FRIENDS

Handsome he's not!
No, in good truth!

Bello non è,
in verità.

BUTTERFLY
(*offended*)

Handsomer man
You never saw,
Not in your dreams.

Bello è cosi
che non si può
sognar di più.

THE MOTHER

I think he's fine! | Mi pare un re!

OTHER FRIENDS

He's worth a lot. | Vale un Perù.

FIRST COUSIN
(*to Butterfly*)

Why, Goro offered
Him to me.
But I said no.

Goro l'offrì
pur anche a me.
Ma s'ebbe un no!

BUTTERFLY
(*contemptuously*)

To you, my dear!
A likely tale!

Sì, giusto tu!
Sì, giusto tu!

SOME FRIENDS

Because on her
His choice did fall,
She would look down
Upon us all!

Ecco, perchè
prescelta fu,
vuol far con te
la soprappiù.

OTHER FRIENDS
(*looking pityingly at Butterfly*)

I think her beauty's
On the wane.

La sua beltà
già disfiorì.

SOME FRIENDS

He'll never stay. | Divorzierà.

COUSIN AND ALL RELATIONS AND FRIENDS

I hope he won't. | Spero di sì.

GORO
(*Annoyed at the idle chatter, he goes from one to another, entreating them to lower their voices.*)

For goodness sake
Be silent all.

Per carità
tacete un po' . . .

UNCLE YAKUSIDÉ
(*staring at the servants who are bringing wines and liqueurs*)

Is there no wine? | Vino ce n'è?

THE MOTHER AND THE AUNT
(*peeering around, trying to keep out of sight*)

Let's look around. | Guardiamo un pò.

SOME FRIENDS
(*with satisfaction to Yakusidè*)

I've just seen some
The hue of tea
And crimson too!

Ne vidi già
Color di thè
e chermisi!

*4
YAKUSIDÉ

[Is there no wine? Let's look around!]

Vino ce n'è? Guardiamo un po!

GORO
(*again intervening to stop the noise, and then making signs that they should be quiet*)

[For goodness sake, be silent all.]

Per carità, tacete un po'!

SOME FRIENDS
(*At Goro's signals, the relations and guests gather in groups, still fidgeting and chattering*)

[He offered him to me also,
but I replied: 'I don't want him!'
Without much looking
I will find better ones
and I will say no to them!]

Ei l'offri pur anco a me,
ma risposi: Non lo vo'!
Senza tanto ricercar
io ne trovo dei miglior,
e gli dirò di no!

OTHER FRIENDS

[He is handsome, he seems a king to me!
I would not have replied no!
I would never have said no!
No, my dear
he's certainly a fine gentleman —
I would never say no to him!]

Egli è bel, mi pare un re!
Non avrei riposto no!
Non direi mai no!
No, mia cara
è davvero un gran signor
ne gli mai direi di no!

PINKERTON

Ah, she's a gem, a flower,
which in good faith I have gathered.
Her fascinating presence
Fans the flame of my passion.

Si, è vero, è un fiore, un fiore,
e in fede mia l'ho colto.
L'esotico suo adore
m'ha il cervello sconvolto.

(*He points to Butterfly.*)

SHARPLESS
(*to Pinkerton*)

Indeed, my friend, you're lucky!

O amico fortunato!

O trebly lucky Pinkerton
Since Fate has let you gather
A flower hardly opened.

[13]

O Pinkerton fortunato
che in sorte v'è toccato
un fior pur or sbocciato!

I have never seen fairer,
Nor sweeter maiden than
This little Butterfly

Non più bella e d'assai
fanciulla io vidi mai
di questa Butterfly.

Do not look on this contract
And on her faith as folly,
Be careful, for she believes you.

E se a voi sembran scede
il patto e la sua fede
badate! . . . Ella ci crede.

BUTTERFLY
(*to her mother*)

Mother, come here.

Mamma, vien qua.

(*to the others*)

Listen to me:
all of you look,
one, two, three,
all of you down!

Badate a me:
attenti, orsù,
uno — due — tre
e tutti giù.

(*At a sign from Butterfly they all kow-tow to Pinkerton and Sharpless.*)

---

*4 These four speeches, and the opening sequence of the next scene (Goro and the Commissioner/Registrar, Pinkerton and the Relations) were cut after the first performance. In fact the whole of that scene of introductions clearly bothered Puccini and was rewritten twice before he finally cut it in the 1906 Paris version.

(*Meanwhile, Goro has made the servants bring out some small tables, on which they place a variety of cakes, sweetmeats, drinks and tea things. To one side they set some cushions and a small table with writing materials. The friends and relations express pleasure at the sight of refreshments. Goro brings the Comissioner and the Registrar forward.*)

GORO

[Here Mr Registrar. And here, Excellency. I have the pleasant task of expressing to you, not merely in words but in the American way, the appreciation of . . .]	Qui signor Ufficiale. E qui Eccelenza. Ho la dolce incombenza di esprimervi non già col parlar vano ma all'uso americano la grata intenzion del qui presente . . .
(*giving them some bank notes*)	
[. . . Mr Lieutenant here.]	. . . signor Luogotenente.

THE COMMISSIONER AND THE REGISTRAR

[Very good.] — Ottimamente.

THE RELATIONS

(*At a sign from Butterfly they advance and bow deeply to Pinkerton*)

[Let us make a deep bow.] — Facciamo un inchino profondo.

(*They repeat the bow.*)

[And we make a second one.] — E noi ne facciamo un secondo.

PINKERTON

(*bowing again*)

[I return it in the same coin.] — La stessa moneta vi do.

THE RELATIONS

(*making a third bow*)

[We will never render you as much honour
as you deserve.]

Giammai non daremo al divino
tuo merto condegna onoranza.

PINKERTON

(*thanking them but indicating that there has been enough bowing*)

[I admire your dedication
but my back won't bend any more.]

Ammiro la vostra costanza
ma il dorso curvar più non so.

(*Butterfly presents her close relations to Pinkerton.*)

BUTTERFLY

[My mother.] — Mia Madre.

PINKERTON

[Very happy.]† — Assai felice.

THE MOTHER

Your Augustness dazzles me with fairness. — Vostra Grazia ha lo splendor del giglio.

BUTTERFLY

My cousin and her son. — Mia cugina e suo figlio.

PINKERTON

(*giving the child a playful smack; the latter draws back timidly*)

He bids fair to grow sturdy! — È ben piantato — promette.

THE CHILD §

(*bowing*)

Your Augustness. — Eccellenza!

---

† This reply was altered to:

Most charmed to meet you. — Riverenza.

§ This line was given to the Cousin for the Brescia production (1904).

BUTTERFLY

My uncle Yakusidé.

Lo zio Yakusidé.

PINKERTON
(*laughing loudly*)

Is that he? Ha! Ha!

È quello? . . . Ah! ah!

RELATIONS AND FRIENDS
(*pushing Yakusidé forward*)

Yakusidé . . . Ha! Ha!

Yakusidé . . . Ah! Ah!

YAKUSIDÉ
(*laughing, then obsequiously to Pinkerton*)

Eh! Eh!
Your antecedents shall live for ever!

Eh! Eh!
Salute agli avi e gloriose gesta.

SOME RELATIONS

May the Heavens smile upon thee.

Buona vista ai tuoi occhi.

OTHERS

May your path be strewn with roses.

Buone pianelle ai piedi e il cielo in testa.

(*Pinkerton thanks them and, to get rid of them, shows them the delicacies spread out. The friends and relations rush to the tables; the servants hand round saki, sweets, pastries, and drinks; lively exclamations from the guests. Butterfly seats her mother and cousin close to her, trying to restrain their greediness. Sharpless invites the Commissioner and the Official to come forward again; he introduces Pinkerton to them and vice versa.*)

SHARPLESS

Sir Francis Blummy Pinkerton,
His Lordship the Imperial Commissioner . . .

Sir Francis Blummy Pinkerton
Sua Grazia il Commissario Imperiale . . .

THE COMMISSIONER

Takasago.

Takasago.

SHARPLESS

And the State's registration official.

Dello Stato Civil l'Ufficiale.

THE OFFICIAL

Hanako.

Hanako.

(*Goro accompanies the Consul, the Commissioner and the Registrar to the table with writing materials. The Consul examines the papers and gets the contract ready. Pinkerton draws near to Butterfly and gently offers her some sweets.*)

PINKERTON

For my beloved.

All' amor mio!

(*seeing that Butterfly appears embarrassed*)

Do sweets displease you?

Vi spiacciono i confetti?

*[5]

BUTTERFLY
(*rising*)

Mister F.B. Pinkerton, forgive me . . .

Signor F.B. Pinkerton, perdono . . .

(*She holds out her arms which are encumbered by stuffed-out sleeves.*)

May I show you a young girl's few
Possessions?

Io vorrei . . . pochi oggetti
da donna . . .

---

*[5] In the 1906 version the preceding scene was omitted and the act continued with these lines, after Pinkerton had led Butterfly towards the house and the guests had dispersed in the garden. (They replaced those in the earlier text.)

PINKERTON

Come my beloved.

Vieni, amor mio!

(*seeing that Butterfly appears embarrassed*)

D'you like our little home?

Vi piace la casetta?

PINKERTON

But where are they? | Dove sono?

BUTTERFLY
(pointing to her sleeves)

They are here . . . do you mind them? | Sono qui . . . vi dispiace?

PINKERTON
(Rather astonished, he smiles, then quickly and gallantly reassures her.)

Why should I mind, | O perchè mai,
My lovely Butterfly? | mia bella Butterfly?

BUTTERFLY
(She empties her sleeves, placing their contents one by one on a stool.)

Silken kerchiefs . . . For smoking . . . A coloured ribbon. | Fazzoletti. — La pipa. — Una cintura.
A little silver buckle . . . | Un piccolo fermaglio. —
And a mirror . . . and a fan . . . | Uno specchio. — Un ventaglio.

PINKERTON
(He sees a jar.)

What is that you have? | Quel barattolo?

BUTTERFLY

It's just a jar of carmine. | Un vaso di tintura.

PINKERTON

For shame! | Ohibò!

BUTTERFLY

You don't like it? | Vi spiace? . . .
(She throws away the pot of rouge.)
There! | Via!

(She draws forth a long narrow sheath.)

PINKERTON

And that? | E quello?

BUTTERFLY
(very gravely)

That I hold most sacred. | Cosa sacra è mia.

PINKERTON
(curiously)

And am I not to see it? | E non si può veder?

BUTTERFLY
(Beseeching and grave, she lays down the sheath very reverently.)

Not just now. | C'è troppa gente.
Please forgive me. | Perdonate.

GORO
(who has approached, whispers to Pinkerton)

It was sent by | È un presente
The Mikado to her father, with a message . . . | del Mikado a suo padre . . . coll'invito . . .

(He imitates the action of suicide.)

PINKERTON
(softly to Goro)

And her father? | E . . . suo padre?

GORO

Was obedient. [12] | Ha obbedito.

(He withdraws, mingling with the guests.)

BUTTERFLY

(*She takes some tiny statuettes from her sleeves and shows them to Pinkerton.*)

The Ottokē.	Gli Ottokē.

PINKERTON

(*He takes one and examines it with curiosity.*)

These small figures? But what are they?	Quei pupazzi? . . . Avete detto?

BUTTERFLY

The souls of my forefathers.	Son l'anime degli avi.

PINKERTON

Ah! I bow before them.	Ah! . . . il mio rispetto.

(*He puts down the images, then rises.*)

BUTTERFLY

(*She leads Pinkerton to one side and speaks to him confidentially.*)

Hear what I must tell you:	Ieri sono salita
All alone I went softly to the Mission.	tutta sola in secreto alla Missione.
[I do not know the best way to say	*6 Dir ben non saprei
Whether I could see clearly what was right or wrong:	se del bene o del mal chiaro discerno:
We pray to many gods,	noi preghiam mille Dei,
You pray to a single god,	voi pregate un sol Dio
Powerful and everlasting.]	grande ed eterno.
No-one knows what I have done,	Lo zio Bonzo nol sa,
Neither friends nor relations. My fate I have to follow,	né i miei lo sanno. Io seguo il mio destino
And full of humble faith,	e piena d'umiltà
I bow before the God of Mister Pinkerton.	al Dio del'signor Pinkerton m'inchino.
For me you paid a hundred Yen,	Per me spendeste cento
But I shall try to be most frugal.	en, ma vivrò con molta economia.
And in order to please you	É per farvi contento
I shall try to forget my race and kindred!	potrò quasi obliar la gente mia.

(*She goes to pick up the statuettes.*)

Away they go!	E questi: via!

(*She cuts short her cry, alarmed lest her relations should have heard her, and throws the Ottokē down. Meanwhile Goro has approached the Consul and, having received his orders, thunders forth in stentorian tones.*)

---

*6 The lines in square brackets were cut in 1904 for the second performance at Brescia. The whole soliloquy was reworded for Paris in 1906, as follows:

BUTTERFLY

Entering on my new life,	Colla nuova mia vita
I wish to adopt another religion.	posso adottare nuova religione.

(*timidly*)

No-one knows what I have done,	Lo zio Bonze nol sa,
Neither friends nor relations.	né i miei lo sanno.
My fate I have to follow,	Io seguo il mio destino
And full of humble faith	e piena d'umiltà
I bow before the God of Mister Pinkerton.	al Dio del signor Pinkerton m'inchino.
The Fates have willed	E mio destino
[That I should kneel in the same church	Nella stessa chiesetta in ginocchio
As you, and pray to the same God.]	con voi pregherò lo stesso Dio.
And in order to please you	E per farvi contento
I shall try to forget my race and kindred!	potrò forse obliar la gente mia.
For you my love!	Amore mio!

(*She throws herself into Pinkerton's arms. She stops herself as if afraid that she will be overheard by the relations. Meanwhile, Goro has opened the* shosi *— Sharpless and the officials are in the room where everything is ready for the wedding — Butterfly goes into the house and kneels down: Pinkerton stands next to her — the relations are kneeling in the garden, facing the house.*)

GORO

Silence! Silence!	Tutti zitti!

(*The chattering ceases: they all stop eating and drinking and come forward in a circle, listening with much interest. Pinkerton and Butterfly stand in the centre.*)

THE COMMISSIONER
(*reading out*)

Leave is given to the undersigned, Sir Francis Blummy Pinkerton, Lieutenant serving on the gunboat *Abra'm Lincoln*, of the United States Navy Of North America: And to the spinster known as Butterfly From the district of Omara Nagasaki Hitherto single, and in consequence Never divorced, To join in the bonds of wedlock; to wit The former of his free accord and will. The bride . . .	È concesso al nominato Sir Francis Blummy Pinkerton, Luogotenente nella cannoniera *Lincoln*, marina degli Stati Uniti, America del Nord: ed alla damigella Butterfly del quartiere di Omara-Nagasaki, finor non maritata e in conseguenza non divorziata mai, di unirsi in matrimonio, per diritto il primo, della propria volontà, ed ella . . .

(*Uncle Yakusidé and the child are caught in the act of plunging their hands among the cakes, to the horror of the relations.*)

RELATIONS

Hou! hou! hou! hou!	Hou! hou! hou! hou!

COUSIN
(*scolding the child*)

[I will never take you out again.]	Non ti conduco più.

THE COMMISSIONER
(*Annoyed, he continues with raised voice.*)

. . . the bride with consent of her relations, Witnesses of the contract.	. . . ed ella per consenso dei parenti qui testimoni all'atto.

(*He hands the contract for signature.*)

GORO
(*ceremoniously*)

The bridegroom.	Lo sposo.

(*Pinkerton signs.*)

Now the bride.	Poi la sposa.

(*Butterfly signs.*)

And all is settled.	E tutto è fatto.

Footnote [6] continued (1906).

GORO

Silence! Silence!	Tutti zitti!

THE COMMISSIONER
(*reading out*)

Leave is given to the undersigned, Benjamin Franklin Pinkerton, Lieutenant serving on the gunboat *Abra'm Lincoln*, of the United States Navy Of North America: And to the spinster known as Butterfly From the district of Omara Nagasaki To join in bonds of wedlock. To wit The former, of his free accord and will. The bride with consent of her relations. Witnesses of the contract.	È concesso al nominato Benjamin Franklin Pinkerton, Luogotenente nella cannoniera *Lincoln*, marina degli Stati Uniti, America del Nord: ed alla damigella Butterfly del quartiere di Omara-Nagasaki, di unirsi in matrimonio, per diritto il primo, della propria volontà, . . . ed ella per consenso dei parenti qui testimoni all'atto.

(*He hands the contract for signature.*)

The scene continues, after Goro's three injunctions (see 1904 text), in the note on page 86.

(*The relations hasten to sign; the friends cluster round Butterfly congratulating her.*)

THE GIRL-FRIENDS

Dear Madam Butterfly. — Madama Butterfly!

BUTTERFLY
(*correcting them*)

No. Mrs F.B. Pinkerton. — Madama F.B. Pinkerton.

(*The Registrar removes the contract and informs the Commissioner that everything is completed.*)

THE COMMISSIONER
(*taking leave of Pinkerton*)

Congratulations. — Auguri molti.

PINKERTON

I thank you most sincerely. — I miei ringraziamenti.

THE COMMISSIONER
(*to the Consul*)

May I ask, are you leaving? — Il signor Consul scende?

SHARPLESS

I'll go with you. — L'accompagno.

THE REGISTRAR
(*taking leave of Pinkerton*)

A son and heir. — Posterità.

PINKERTON

I'll do my best. — Mi proverò.

SHARPLESS
(*shaking Pinkerton's hand*)

Be careful! — Giudizio!

We shall meet tomorrow. — Ci vedrem domattina.

Footnote [6] continued. (1906)

THE GIRL-FRIENDS

Dear Madam Butterfly! — Madama Butterfly!

BUTTERFLY
(*gestures with her hands, correcting them with raised finger.*)

No. Mrs B.F. Pinkerton. — Madam B.F. Pinkerton.

(*The girl-friends are making much of Butterfly, who kisses them all: meanwhile the Registrar removes the contract and informs the Commissioner that everything is completed.*)

THE COMMISSIONER
(*congratulating Pinkerton*)

Congratulations. — Auguri molti.

PINKERTON

I thank you most sincerely. — I miei ringraziamenti.

THE COMMISSIONER
(*to the Consul*)

May I ask, are you leaving? — Il signor Console scende?

SHARPLESS

I'll go with you. — L'accompagno.
(*nodding to Pinkerton*)
We shall meet tomorrow. — Ci vedremo domani.

PINKERTON

Until tomorrow. — A meraviglia.

PINKERTON

Tomorrow, surely. | A meraviglia.

(*Pinkerton accompanies the three as far as the path which leads down to the town, and waves his hand to them as they vanish from sight. They had first to pass between two files of friends and relatives, who saluted them with many ceremonious bows. Butterfly has withdrawn close to her mother. Pinkerton returns and is naturally anxious to get rid of the wedding guests.*)

(Now quickly to get rid of
This little family party! How shall I do it?) | (Ed eccoci in famiglia.
Sbrighiamoci al più presto — in modo onesto).

This way, good uncle. | *7 Qua, signor Zio.

(*gaily to Yakusidé, mixing him a whisky*)

Here, the stirrup cup for you I'm mixing. | Il bicchier della staffa.

YAKUSIDÉ

Yes rather! Let's have twenty! | Magari due dozzine!

PINKERTON
(*giving him the bottle*)

And here's the whisky bottle. | E allora la caraffa.

YAKUSIDÉ
(*pompously*)

Drink up your saki and kneel to the Almighty. | Bevi il tuo saki e a Dio piega il ginocchio.

PINKERTON
(*He is about to mix a drink for Butterfly's mother.*)

Here's some for you . . . | La suocera . . .

BUTTERFLY
(*She stops him from pouring out the drink.*)

No, thank you. | Non beve.

Footnote [6] continued. (1906)

THE REGISTRAR
(*congratulating Pinkerton*)

A son and heir. | Posterità.

PINKERTON

I'll do my best. | Mi proverò.

(*The Consul, the Commissioner and the Registrar depart to go down to the town. Sharpless returns and addresses Pinkerton with significance.*)

SHARPLESS

Be careful! | Giudizio!

(*Pinkerton reassures him with a gesture and gives him a friendly wave of the hand.*)

PINKERTON
(*He returns rubbing his hands and talking under his breath.*)

(And now for the family.) | (Ed eccoci in famiglia.)

(*The servants bring in bottles of saki and distribute glasses among the guests.*)

Now to get rid of them quickly — how shall I do it? | Sbrighiamoci al più presto — in modo onesto.

(*He proposes a toast to the guests.*)

Hip! hip! | Hip! hip!

---

*7 This scene was shortened in two stages. In 1904, immediately after the first performance, the whole sequence including Yakusidé's song from 'È l'ora del tramonto' to 'la bottiglia!' was cut. The previous part of the scene was retained for Brescia (etc.) until it was cut altogether in 1906 for Paris. The Paris version thus moved directly from Pinkerton's 'in modo onesto' to his toast 'Hip! hip!' and 'O Kami! O Kami!', and this was interrupted by the off-stage cries of the Bonze, who entered preceded by two men carrying lanterns, and followed by two priests.

PINKERTON
(*offering refreshments all round*)

And the friends
And relations . . . Take some cakes and a glass
Of sherry.

le amiche — due confetti ed un bicchiere
di porto.

YAKUSIDÉ
(*coming forward eagerly*)

Thanks, with pleasure.

Con piacere!

THE GIRL-FRIENDS
(*They drive Yakusidé away.*)

Oh, the drunkard! Oh, the drunkard!

Il beone, il beone!

GORO
(*to Pinkerton, so that he may not encourage the drunkard too much*)

Gently, sir, gently, sir, gently!
Give him a chance and he'd drink up the ocean.

Piano, signore, piano!
ch'egli berrebbe il gran padre oceano!

PINKERTON
(*to the child, giving him a lot of sweets*)

Your turn, young rascal;
Spread out your hands and stuff up your sleeves
With cakes and sweetmeats and lots of pastry.

A te marmocchio;
spalanca le tue maniche ed insacca
chicche e pasticci a macca.

(*He takes a glass and raises it.*)

Hip! Hip!

Ip! Ip!

ALL
(*toasting*)

O Kami! O Kami! [14] O Kami! O Kami!

PINKERTON

Now drink to the newly married couple!

E beviamo ai novissimi legami.

ALL

O Kami! O Kami!

O Kami! O Kami!

BUTTERFLY
(*disapproving and timidly to Pinkerton*)

[It is the hour of sunset . . .

È l'ora del tramonto . . .

PINKERTON

Uncle, I want a song.

Zio, voglio una canzone.

(*Butterfly, annoyed, wants to prevent her uncle from singing, but does not dare.*)

YAKUSIDÉ

Here I am, quite ready.

Eccomi pronto.

(*Pinkerton sits down in an armchair and encourages Yakusidé to sing.*)

In the shade of a Keki
On Nunki-Nunko-Yama,
The day of the Goseki
When all the girls are beautiful,
The day of the Goseki
On Nunki-Nunko-Yama,
In the shade of a Keki.

All'ombra d'un Kekì
sul Nunki-Nunko-Yama,
il di del Goseki
quante fanciulle belle,
il di del Goseki
sul Nunki-Nunko-Yama,
all'ombra d'un Kekì.

(*to Pinkerton*)

Do you like it?

Vi piace?

PINKERTON

Very moving. Go on, start again.

Commovente. Va, ripiglia.

YAKUSIDE

In the shade of a Keki	All'ombra d'un Keki
On Nunki-Nunko-Yama,	sul Nunki-Nunko-Yama,
The day of the Goseki	il di del Goseki
O beautiful ones, what are you doing there,	o che ci fate o belle,
The day of the Goseki	il di del Goseki
On Nunki-Nunko-Yama,	sul Nunki-Nunko-Yama,
In the shade . . .	all'ombra . . .

(*He interrupts himself, shouting.*)

The bottle! . . .]	la bottiglia! . . .

(*He notices that the child has taken the bottle of whisky and is raising it to his mouth, and he chases after him amid general laughter. Suddenly a strange figure appears from below, at the sight of whom everyone is astonished. It is the Bonze, who comes forward furiously, and at the sight of Butterfly, stretches out his hands threateningly towards her, shouting.*)

THE BONZE

Cho-Cho-San! Cho-Cho-San!	[15] Cio-Cio-San! . . . Cio-Cio-San!
My curse upon you.	Abominazione!

(*At this shout, all the relations and friends are thunderstruck and huddle together in terror: Butterfly remains in a corner.*)

GORO

(*annoyed at the Bonze's arrival*)

A curse on this intruder!	Un corno al guastafeste!
What on earth brought him hither	Chi ci leva d'intorno
Of all troublesome people? . . .	le persone moleste?! . . .

(*He signs to the servants to take away the tables, stools and cushions; then prudently retires, grumbling furiously.*)

ALL

It's her uncle!	Lo zio Bonzo!

THE BONZE

(*to Butterfly, who stands isolated from the rest*)

What were	Che hai
You doing at the Mission?	tu fatto alla Missione?

PINKERTON

(*angry at the scene made by the Bonze*)

What's that lunatic shouting?	Che mi strilla quel matto?

THE BONZE

I ask you, what were you doing?	Rispondi, che hai tu fatto?

ALL

(*anxiously, turning to Butterfly*)

Give answer, Cho-Cho-San!	Rispondi Cio-Cio-San!

THE BONZE

How then, don't you even falter?	Come, hai tu gli occhi asciutti?
Are these the fruits of evil?	Son questi dunque i frutti?

(*shouting*)

She has renounced us all!	Ci ha rinnegato tutti!

ALL

(*scandalized, shouting long and loud*)

Hou! Cho-Cho-San!	Hou! Cio-Cio-San!

THE BONZE

She's renounced, let me tell you,	Rinnegato, vi dico,
Her true religion.	degli avi il culto antico.

ALL

Hou! Cho-Cho-San!

Hou! Cio-Cio-San!

(*Butterfly hides her face in her hands.*)

THE BONZE
(*hurling curses at Butterfly*)

Kami sarundasico!
And may the Gods condemn you
To eternal damnation!

Kami sarundasico!
All'anima tua guasta
qual supplizio sovrasta!

(*Butterfly's mother comes forward to protect her but the Bonze pushes her away roughly and approaches Butterfly in a fury, shouting in her face.*)

PINKERTON
(*He has lost his patience and intervenes between the Bonze and Butterfly.*)

That's quite enough, d'you hear me?

Ehi, dico: basta, basta!

(*At the sound of Pinkerton's voice the Bonze stops short in amazement, then with a sudden resolve he invites relations and friends to come away.*)

THE BONZE

Come with me all — we'll leave her!

Venite tutti. — Andiamo!

(*to Butterfly*)

She has renounced us all . . .

Ci ha rinnegato e noi . . .

ALL
(*They retire to the back with arms outstretched pointing at Butterfly.*)

And we renounce you!
Hou! Cio-Cio-San!
Kami sarundasico!

[15] Ti rinneghiamo!
Hou! Cio-Cio-San!
Kami sarundasico!

PINKERTON
(*authoritatively*)

Leave my house, I command you. Here
I'm the master. I'll have no curses and no
disturbances here.

Sbarazzate all'istante. In casa mia
niente baccano e niente bonzeria.

(*At Pinkerton's words, they all rush hastily towards the path which leads down to the town: Butterfly's mother again tries to approach her but is dragged away by the others. The Bonze disappears down the path to the temple, followed by his acolytes. The shouts gradually grow fainter. Butterfly remains silent and motionless, her face in her hands, while Pinkerton goes to the top of the path to make sure that all these troublesome guests have gone. Butterfly bursts into childish tears. Pinkerton hears her and anxiously hastens to her side, supporting her as she is fainting, and tenderly takes her hands from her face.*)

Dearest, my dearest, weep no more.
All their shouting means nothing.

Bimba, bimba, non piangere
per gracchiar di ranocchi.

BUTTERFLY
(*She holds her ears so as not to hear the shouts.*)

Oh, how they curse!

Urlano ancor!

PINKERTON
(*cheering her*)

All your respected tribe
And all the Bonzes in Japan are not worth
A tear from those sweet almond eyes
I love so.

Tutta la tua tribù
e i Bonzi tutti del Giappon non valgono
il pianto di quegli occhi
cari e belli.

BUTTERFLY
(*smiling with childlike pleasure*)

Indeed? I'll weep no more.

Davver? Non piango più.

(*Evening begins to fall.*)

And now I do not care that I'm deserted
For your words have brought comfort
And they fall like gentle balm on my heart.

E quasi del ripudio non mi duole
per le vostre parole
che mi suonan così dolci nel cuor.

(*She stoops to kiss Pinkerton's hand.*)

PINKERTON
(*gently stopping her*)

What's this? My hand? | Che fai? . . . la man?

BUTTERFLY

They tell me
That abroad, where the people are more cultured,
This is a token of the highest honour.

Mi han detto
che laggiù fra la gente costumata
è questo il segno del maggior rispetto.

SUZUKI

Izaghi Izanami
sarundasico
Kami
Izaghi and Izanami
sarundasico Kami.

Izaghi ed Izanami
sarundasico, e
Kami,
e Iszaghi ed Izanami
sarundasico, e Kami.

PINKERTON
(*wondering at the subdued murmurs*)

Who's murmuring in there? | Chi brontola lassù?

BUTTERFLY

'Tis Suzuki who offers up her prayer
For the night.

È Suzuki che fa la sua preghiera
seral.

PINKERTON
(*The night draws in more and more, and Pinkerton leads Butterfly to the house.*)

Evening is falling . . . [16] Viene la sera . . .

BUTTERFLY

With shadows and quiet. | . . . e l'ombra e la quiete.

PINKERTON

You're here alone — | E sei qui sola.

BUTTERFLY

Alone and renounced.
They've renounced me, still I'm happy!

Sola e rinnegata!
Rinnegata e felice!

PINKERTON
(*He claps his hands three times — the servants and Suzuki hurry in.*)

Suzuki, the screen. | A voi — chiudete.

(*The servants silently slide several partitions along.*)

BUTTERFLY
(*with deep feeling to Pinkerton*)

Yes, we are all alone . . .
The world is yonder.

Si, si, noi tutti soli . . .
E fuori il mondo.

PINKERTON
(*laughing*)

Your uncle breathing thunder! | E il Bonzo furibondo.

(*He sits down and lights a cigarette.*)

BUTTERFLY
(*to Suzuki, who has come in with the servants and is awaiting orders*)

Suzuki, bring me my garments. | Suzuki, le mie vesti.

(*Suzuki rummages in a chest and gives Butterfly her night attire and a small box of toilet requisites.*)

SUZUKI
(*bowing low to Pinkerton*)

Good night, Sir. | Buona notte.

(*Pinkerton claps his hands; the servants run away. Butterfly retires to a corner at the back and, assisted by Suzuki, carefully performs her toilet for the night, exchanging her wedding-garment for one of pure white; then she sits down on a cushion and, looking in a small hand-mirror, arranges her hair. Suzuki goes out.*)

BUTTERFLY

I'm glad to be rid of This cumbersome obi, . . . A bride should be robed in A garment of white. He's peeping and smiling, Pretends not to see me. He'll see that I'm blushing. I wish I could hide! I know his angry voice Still shouting curses . . . Butterfly . . . they've renounced me . . . They've renounced me, yet I'm happy.	Quest'obi pomposa di sciogliermi tarda . . . si vesta la sposa di puro candor. Tra motti sommessi sorride . . . mi guarda. Celarmi potessi! ne ho tanto rossor! E ancor dentro l'irata voce mi maledice . . . Butterfly . . . rinnegata . . . Rinnegata . . . e felice.

PINKERTON

(*lounging in the wicker chair, watching Butterfly amorously*)

Why, all her pretty movements Are like a little squirrel's. To think that pretty creature Is my wife! My wife!	Con moti di scoiattolo i nodi allenta e scioglie! Pensar che quel giocattolo è mia moglie. Mia moglie!

(*smiling*)

But her charm is So alluring, my heart Is beating madly With passionate longing!	Ma tale muliebre grazia dispiega, ch'io mi struggo per la febbre d'un subito desio.

(*He stands up and gradually approaches Butterfly with outstretched arms.*)

Child, from whose eyes the witchery is shining, Now you are all my own. You're dressed all in white like a lily. Your ebony tresses are shining On ivory shoulders.	[17] Bimba dagli occhi pieni di malia, ora sei tutta mia. Sei tutta vestita di giglio. Mi piace la treccia tua bruna fra i candidi veli . . .

BUTTERFLY

(*She descends from the terrace, followed by Pinkerton.*)

I come like The Moon's little Goddess, The little Moon-Goddess who comes down by night from Her bridge in a sky full of stars!	Somiglio la piccola Dea della luna, la Dea della luna che scende la notte dal ponte del ciel . . .

PINKERTON

Bewitching all mortals . . .	E affascina i cuori . . .

BUTTERFLY

Then she takes them, And she folds them in mantle of white, Away she bears them To realms high above.	E li prende, li avvolge nel bianco mantel. E via se li reca al diletto suo nido, negli alti reami.

PINKERTON

But dear one, as yet you haven't told me, You still haven't told me you love me. D'you think that my Goddess knows The sweet words I am longing to hear?	Ma intanto finor non m'hai detto, ancor non m'hai detto che m'ami. Le sa quella Dea le parole che appagan gli ardenti desir?

BUTTERFLY

She knows, but perhaps will not tell you For fear she may die of her love!	Le sa. Forse dirle non vuole per tema d'averne a morir!

Yasuko Hayashi as Cio-Cio-San and José Carreras as Pinkerton at Covent Garden in 1978 (photo: Donald Southern)

Raina Kabaivanska as Cio-Cio-San and Dennis O'Neill as Pinkerton at Covent Garden in 1981 (photo: Christina Burton)

PINKERTON

Fear not, my dearest, for love does not mean dying,
No, it's living, and it smiles
Like a joy born in Heaven.
I see it shine, as in your eyes, dearest, I'm gazing.

Stolta paura, l'amor non uccide
ma dà vita, e sorride
per gioie celestiali
come ora fa nei tuoi lunghi occhi ovali.

(*He draws close to Butterfly and takes her face in his hands.*)

BUTTERFLY *[8]

(*With a sudden movement, she withdraws from Pinkerton's ardent embrace; reticently*)

I used to think: if anyone should want me . . .

Pensavo: se qualcuno mi volesse . . .

(*She stops short.*)

PINKERTON

Why do you falter?

Perchè t'arresti? Andiamo . . . su, racconta.

BUTTERFLY
(*resuming, simply*)

I used to think: if anyone should want me
Then perhaps for a time I might have married.
'Twas then that the Nakodo
Came to me with your marriage offer but
The truth I must confess:
At the beginning, all he said was useless.
A stranger from America!
A foreigner! A barbarian!
Forgive me, I did not know . . .

. . . pensavo: se qualcuno mi volesse
forse lo sposerei per qualche tempo.
Fu allora che il Nakodo
le vostre nozze ci propose. Ma,
vi dico in verità
a tutta prima le propose invano.
Un uomo americano?
Un barbaro! una vespa! mi dicevo.
Scusate — non sapevo . . .

PINKERTON
(*encouraging her to go on*)

My gentle darling! And then?
Continue . . .

Amor mio dolce! E poi?
Racconta.

BUTTERFLY

But now, beloved,
You are the world, more than the world to me.
Indeed I loved you the very first moment
That I saw you.

Adesso voi
siete per me l'occhio del firmamento.
E mi piaceste dal primo momento
Che vi ho veduto.

(*Butterfly has a sudden panic and puts her hands to her ears, as though she still hears her relatives shouting; then she rallies and once more turns confidingly to Pinkerton.*)

You're so
Strong, so handsome! Your laugh is
So open and so carefree.
You tell me things that I never could dream of.
Yes, I am happy.

— Siete
alto, forte. — Ridete
con modi si palesi!
E dite cose che mai non intesi.
Or son contenta.

(*Night has closed in completely; the sky is unclouded and closely strewn with stars: Butterfly slowly draws nearer to Pinkerton; and then tenderly, almost beseechingly*)

Ah, love me a little, [18]
Oh, just a very little,
As you would love a baby.
It's all that I ask for.
I come of a people
Accustomed to little;
Grateful for love that's silent;
Light as a blossom
And yet everlasting
As the sky, as the fathomless ocean.

— Vogliatemi bene,
un bene piccolino,
un bene da bambino
quale a me si conviene.
Noi siamo gente avvezza
alle piccole cose
umili e silenziose,
ad una tenerezza
sfiorante e pur profonda
come il ciel, come l'onda del mare.

*[8] This explanation was cut in 1906: 'Pensavo: se qualcuno . . .' to 'Adesso voi . . .'

PINKERTON

Give me your hands that I may softly kiss them.	Dammi ch'io baci le tue mani care.

(*He exclaims, tenderly.*)

My Butterfly! What a good name they gave you,	Mia Butterfly! . . . come t'han ben nomata
Fragile thing of beauty.	tenue farfalla . . .

BUTTERFLY

(*At these words Butterfly's face clouds over and she withdraws her hands.*)

Ah, but in your country [15]	Dicon che oltre mare
If a butterfly is caught by man	se cade in man dell'uom, ogni farfalla
(*with an expression of fear*)	
He'll pierce its heart with a needle	da uno spillo è trafitta
(*with anguish*)	
And then leave it to perish!	ed in tavola infitta!

PINKERTON

(*taking her hands again gently and smiling*)

In that there is some truth	Un po' di vero c'è.
And shall I tell you why?	E lo sai tu perchè?
It never can escape.	Perchè non fugga più.
(*with ardour, caressing her affectionately*)	
See, I have caught you . . .	Io t'ho ghermita . . .
I hold you as you flutter.	Ti serro palpitante.
You're mine.	Sei mia.

BUTTERFLY

(*She throws herself into his arms.*)

Yes, yours for ever.	Sì, per la vita.

PINKERTON

Come then, come then . . .	Vieni, vieni.
(*Butterfly draws back, as though ashamed of having been too bold.*)	
Love, what fear holds you trembling?	Via dall'anima in pena
Have done with all misgivings.	l'angoscia paurosa.
(*He points to the starlit sky.*)	
The starlight is shining	È notte serena!
And the world lies a-sleeping!	Guarda: dorme ogni cosa!

BUTTERFLY

(*looking at the sky, enraptured*)

Ah! Night of wonder! Stars unending!	[9] Ah! Dolce notte! Quante stelle!
I have never seen such glory!	Non le vidi mai sì belle!
Throbbing, sparkling, each star in heaven,	Trema, brilla ogni favilla
Like a fiery eye is flashing.	col baglior d'una pupilla.
Oh! How shining are the heavens;	[10] Oh! quanti occhi fissi, attenti
Every star that shines afar	d'ogni parte a riguardar!
Is gazing on us,	Pei firmamenti,
Lighting the future for us . . .	via pei lidi, via pel mare . . .
See the stars!	Quanti sguardi!
Thy perfect calm is breathing	Tutto estatico d'amor
Love near and far!	ride il ciel . . .

PINKERTON

(*with passionate longing*)

Ah! Come, beloved.	Vieni, vieni! . . .

(*They go up from the garden into the house.*)

The curtain falls.

Pinkerton (Arthur Servent) waits for his bride on their wedding night in the Sadler's Wells 1945 production (photo: Angus McBean, © Harvard Theatre Collection)

Act Two

Inside Butterfly's House

The curtain rises: the room is in semi-darkness. Suzuki, kneeling before the image of the Buddha, is praying. From time to time she rings the prayer-bell. Butterfly is standing rigid and motionless near a screen. [15]

SUZUKI
(*praying*)

Izaghi, Izanami,	E Izaghi ed Izanami,
Sarundasico, Kami . . .	Sarundasico e Kami . . .

(*stopping short*)

My head is throbbing!	Oh! la mia testa!

(*She rings the bell to invoke the attention of the Gods.*)

And thou,	E tu,
Ten-Sjoo-daj!	Ten-Sjoo-daj!

(*in a tearful voice, looking at Butterfly*)

Grant me that Butterfly	Fate che Butterfly
Shall weep no more, no more, no more!	non pianga più, mai più, mai più, mai più!

BUTTERFLY
(*without moving*)

The Gods of Japan [8b]	Pigri ed obesi
Are uncaring and lazy!	son gli Dei Giapponesi.
The God my husband prays to will give an answer	L'americano Iddio son persuasa
Far more quickly to those who bow before him.	ben più presto risponde a chi l'implori.
But I'm afraid he's silent	Ma temo ch'egli ignori
For we're so far away here.	che noi stiam qui di casa.

(*She remains pensive. Suzuki rises and slides back the partition at the back leading to the garden.*)

Suzuki, how soon shall we be starving?	Suzuki, è lungi la miseria?

SUZUKI
(*She goes to a small cabinet and opens a casket to look for some money. She goes to Butterfly and shows her a very few coins.*)

This is	Questo è
All that is left us.	l'ultimo fondo.

BUTTERFLY

No more? Oh, we have been careless. [8b, 15, 1]	Questo? Oh! Troppe spese!

SUZUKI
(*She puts the money back into the cabinet which she closes, sighing.*)

Unless he comes, and quickly,	S'egli non torna e presto,
We'll have nothing to live on.	siamo male in arnese.

BUTTERFLY
(*with decision*)

He'll come, though.	Ma torna.

SUZUKI
(*shaking her head*)

Will he come?	Tornerà!

BUTTERFLY
(*vexed, approaching Suzuki*)

Why did he order	Perchè dispone
The Consul to provide this dwelling for us?	che il Console provveda alla pigione?
Now answer that!	rispondi, su!

(*Suzuki is silent, Butterfly persists.*) [20, 4]

And why was he so careful	Perchè con tante cure
To have the house provided with safe locks	la casa rifornì di serrature,
If he did not intend to come again?	s'ei non volesse ritornar mai più?

SUZUKI

I don't know!	Non lo so.

BUTTERFLY
(*rather annoyed and surprised at such ignorance*)

You don't know?	Non lo sai?

(*calming down again and with proud confidence*)

Well then I'll tell you, so as to keep out	Io te lo dico. Per tener ben fuori
Those spiteful plagues, my relations, who might annoy me;	le zanzare, i parenti ed i dolori
And inside, just to give	e dentro, con gelosa
To me, his wife, protection, [9]	custodia, la sua sposa
His beloved little wife, Butterfly.	che son io: Butterfly.

SUZUKI
(*still far from convinced*)

I never yet have	Mai non s'è udito
Heard of a foreign husband	di straniero marito
Who did return to his nest.	che sia tornato al nido.

BUTTERFLY
(*furious, seizing hold of Suzuki*)

Ah! Silence, or I'll kill you.	Ah! Taci, o t'uccido.

(*still trying to convince her*)

Why, on the very day he left	Quell'ultima mattina:
I asked — You'll come back to me again?	tornerete signor? — gli domandai.
And with heart so heavy,	Egli, col cuore grosso,
To conceal his sorrow,	per celarmi la pena
Sadly smiling he answered:	sorridendo rispose:

(*with much charm, trying to imitate Pinkerton*)

'O Butterfly,	'O Butterfly
My dearest little darling,	piccina mogliettina,
I'll return in the springtime,	tornerò colle rose
The warm and sunny season	alla stagion serena
When the flowers are in blossom and robins are nesting.'	quando fa la nidiata il pettirosso.'

(*Calm and convinced, she stretches out on the floor.*)

He'll return.	E tornerà.

SUZUKI
(*incredulously*)

We'll hope.	Speriam.

BUTTERFLY
(*insisting*)

Say it with me:	Dillo con me:
He'll return.	Tornerà.

SUZUKI
(*To please her, she repeats the words, but mournfully.*)

He'll return.	Tornerà . . .

(*She bursts into tears.*)

BUTTERFLY
(*surprised*)

Weeping? But why?	Piangi? Perchè?
Have you no faith, Suzuki?	Ah, la fede ti manca!

(*She continues, full of faith, smiling. She acts the scene as though it were actually happening.*)

Listen. One fine day we'll notice [19]	Senti. — Un bel dì, vedremo
A thread of smoke arising on the sea	levarsi un fil di fumo sull'estremo

In the far horizon,	confin del mare.
And then the ship appearing;	E poi la nave appare.
Soon the trim white vessel	E poi la nave bianca
Glides into the harbour, thunders forth her cannon.	Entra nel porto, romba il suo saluto.
See how he is coming!	Vedi? È venuto!
I do not go to meet him. Not I! I stay	Io non gli scendo incontro. Io no. Mi metto
Upon the brow of the hillside and wait there . . . and wait	là sul ciglio del colle e aspetto, e aspetto, e aspetto
For a long time, but never weary	gran tempo e non mi pesa
Of the long waiting.	la lunga attesa.
And from the crowded city see him coming,	E . . . uscito dalla folla cittadina
From far away approaching,	un uomo, un picciol punto
A man is climbing the hillside. [20]	s'avvia per la collina.
Can you guess who it is?	Chi sarà? chi sarà?
And when he's reached the summit,	E come sarà giunto
Can you guess what he'll say?	che dirà? che dirà?
He will call: 'Butterfly' from the distance.	Chiamerà Butterfly dalla lontana.
I, without answering, hold myself	Io senza far risposta
Quietly concealed,	me ne starò nascosta
A bit to tease him and a bit so as not to die [19]	un po' per celia, un po' per non morire
At our first meeting; and then a little troubled	al primo incontro ed egli alquanto in pena
He will call, he will call:	chiamerà, chiamerà:
'My dearest Butterfly —	'Piccina — mogliettina
My little orange blossom!'	olezzo di verbena',
The names he used to call me when he lived here.	i nomi che mi dava al suo venire.

(*to Suzuki*)

This will all come to pass, of that I'm certain.	Tutto questo avverrà, te lo prometto.
Banish your idle fears, for he will	Tienti la tua paura — io son sicura
Return, I know. [19]	fede l'aspetto.

(*Butterfly and Suzuki embrace with emotion. Butterfly dismisses her and she goes out of the door on the left: Butterfly looks after her sadly. Goro and Sharpless appear in the garden* [4]: *Goro looks into the room, sees Butterfly through a window and says to Sharpless, who is following him:*)

GORO

Ah. She's here.	C'è. — Entrate.

(*Goro and Sharpless cross the garden.*) [2, 1]

SHARPLESS

(*He knocks cautiously at the door on the right.*)

Please excuse me.	Chiedo scusa . . .

(*He sees Butterfly, who hearing someone come in, has risen.*)

Madam Butterfly.	Madama Butterfly . . .

BUTTERFLY

(*She corrects him, without turning round.*)

My name is Pinkerton, If you please.	Madama Pinkerton, Prego.

(*She turns, recognises the Consul and claps her hands for joy.*) [4]

Why, here is the Consul!	Oh, il mio signor Console!

(*Suzuki enters eagerly and prepares a small table with smoking equipment, some cushions and a stool.*)

SHARPLESS

(*surprised*)

So you remember?	Mi ravvisate?

BUTTERFLY

(*doing the honours of the house*)

You are welcome, be seated. You're very welcome!	Benvenuto in casa americana.

SHARPLESS

Thank you. [21] Grazie.

BUTTERFLY

(She invites the Consul to sit near the table: Sharpless drops awkwardly on to a cushion: Butterfly sits down on the other side and smiles slyly behind her fan on seeing the Consul's discomfort: then, with great charm, she asks him:)

And your honourable ancestors, — Avi-antenati
Are they well then? — tutti bene?

SHARPLESS

(thanking her with a smile)

I hope so. — Ma spero.

BUTTERFLY

(She signs to Suzuki to prepare the pipe.)

You smoke? — Fumate?

SHARPLESS

Thank you. — Grazie.

(Anxious to explain the object of his visit, he produces a letter from his pocket.)

I've here ... — Ho qui ...

BUTTERFLY

(interrupting him)

Your Honour, the sky — Signore — io vedo
Is quite unclouded. — il cielo azzurro.

(After having taken a draw at the pipe which Suzuki has prepared, she offers it to the Consul.)

SHARPLESS

(refusing)

Thank you ... — Grazie ...

(again trying to resume the thread of his talk)

I've here ... — Ho ...

BUTTERFLY

(She places the pipe on the table and says, very pressingly:)

You prefer — Preferite
Most likely to smoke American ... — forse le sigarette ...

(offering him one)

... cigarettes? — ... Americane?

SHARPLESS

(rather annoyed, taking one)

Well, thank you. — Ma grazie.

(He tries to resume his talk.)

I have to show you ... — Ho da mostrarvi ...

BUTTERFLY

(She hands Sharpless a lighted taper.)

A light? — A voi.

SHARPLESS

(He lights the cigarette but puts it down at once and, showing her the letter, sits on the stool.)

I've a letter — Mi scrisse
From Mister Pinkerton ... — Mr F.B. Pinkerton ...

BUTTERFLY

(very eagerly)

Ah, really? — Davvero!
Is he well? — È un salute?

SHARPLESS

It seems so. — Perfetta.

BUTTERFLY
(*jumping up joyfully*)

Then I am the happiest
Woman in Japan. Would you answer me
A question?

Io son la donna
più lieta del Giappone. — Potrei farvi
una domanda?

(*Suzuki is busy getting tea ready.*)

SHARPLESS

Gladly.

Certo.

BUTTERFLY
(*sits down again*)

At what time
Of the year in America
Do robins nest?

Quando fanno
il lor nido in America
i pettirossi?

SHARPLESS
(*amazed*)

Are you serious?

Come dite?

BUTTERFLY

Yes,
Sooner or later than here?

Si,
prima o dopo di qui?

SHARPLESS

Why d'you ask?

Ma . . . perché?

(*Goro, who is sauntering round the garden, comes up on to the terrace and listens, unseen, to Butterfly.*)

BUTTERFLY

My husband gave his promise
He would return in the joyous season
When robin redbreasts rebuild their nests.
Here they have built them three times already,
But I thought that over there
Robins might not nest so often.

Mio marito m'ha promesso
di ritornar nella stagion beata
che il pettirosso rifa la nidiata.
Qui l'ha rifatta per ben tre volte, ma
può darsi che di là
usi nidiar men spesso.

(*Goro appears and bursts out laughing.*)

BUTTERFLY

Who's laughing?

Chi ride?

(*seeing Goro*)

Oh, it's Goro.

Oh, c'è il Nakodo.

(*softly to Sharpless*)

The wicked fellow.

Un uom cattivo.

GORO
(*bowing obsequiously*)

I was . . .

Godo . . .

BUTTERFLY
(*to Goro, who bows again and goes to help Suzuki*)

Silence.

Zitto.

(*to Sharpless*)

Why, he dared . . .

Egli osò . . .

(*changing her mind*)

No, first I'd like to hear
Your answer to my question.

No, prima rispondete
alla domanda mia.

SHARPLESS
(*confused*)

I am sorry, I can't help you,
I never studied ornithology.

Mi rincresce, ma . . . ignoro . . .
Non ho studiato l'ornitologia.

BUTTERFLY
(*trying to understand*)

Orni . . .	Orni . . .

SHARPLESS

. . . thology.	. . . tologia.

BUTTERFLY

So then you cannot Tell me?	Non lo sapete insomma.

SHARPLESS

No.	No.

(*trying to return to his point*)

We were saying . . .	Dicevamo . . .

BUTTERFLY
(*interrupting him, following her thoughts*)

Ah, yes, (now) Mister Pinkerton had hardly left when Goro Came here and tried to force me, With arguments and presents, To remarry another of his suitors. Now he offers me riches If I will wed an idiot . . .	Ah, si — Goro, appena F.B. Pinkerton fu in mare, mi venne ad assediare con ciarle e con presenti per ridarmi ora questo, or quel marito. Or promette tesori [8b] per uno scimunito . . .

GORO
(*He intervenes, turning to Sharpless and trying to justify himself.*)

The wealthy Yamadori. She's as poor as can be now and all her relatives Have finally renounced her.	Il ricco Yamadori. [15] Ella è povera in canna — I suoi parenti l'han tutti rinnegata.

(*Beyond the terrace Prince Yamadori is seen, followed by two servants carrying flowers.*)

BUTTERFLY
(*She sees Yamadori and points him out to Sharpless, with a smile.*)

Here he is. Now listen.	Eccolo. Attenti.

(*Yamadori enters with great pomp* [21] *from the door on the right, followed by his two servants: Goro and Suzuki run up to him eagerly and go on their hands and knees before him. Then Suzuki takes the flowers and places them in various vases. Yamadori greets the Consul, then bows most graciously to Butterfly. The two Japanese servants, having deposited the flowers, retire to the back, bowing deeply. Goro, servile and officious, places a stool for Yamadori between Sharpless and Butterfly and is very much in evidence during the conversation. Butterfly, Sharpless and Yamadori sit down.*)

Yamadori, and have the throes Of unrequited love not yet released you? Do you still intend to die If I should withhold my kisses?	[22] Yamadori, ancor . . . le pene dell'amor, non v'han deluso? Vi tagliate ancor le vene se il mio bacio vi ricuso?

YAMADORI
(*to Sharpless*)

There is nothing quite so cruel As the pangs of hopeless love.	Tra le cose più moleste è l'inutil sospirar.

BUTTERFLY
(*with graceful raillery*)

You have had so many wives that You should know the feeling well.	Tante mogli omai toglieste, vi doveste abituar.

YAMADORI

Every one of them I married, And divorce has set me free.	Le ho sposate tutte quante e il divorzio mi francò.

BUTTERFLY

Thank you kindly!	Obbligata.

YAMADORI
(*eagerly*)

And yet to you I would swear eternal faith.	A voi però giurerei fede costante.

SHARPLESS
(*Sighing, he replaces the letter in his pocket.*)

(I am very much afraid my message Will not be delivered!)	(Il messaggio, ho gran paura, a trasmetter non riesco.)

GORO
(*indicating Yamadori to Sharpless, with emphasis*)

Houses, servants, treasures, at Omara A truly regal palace.	Ville, servi, oro, il retaggio d'un palazzo principesco!

BUTTERFLY
(*seriously*)

But my hand's bestowed already.	[8a] Già legata è la mia fede.

GORO AND YAMADORI
(*to Sharpless*)

She still thinks she still is married.	Maritata ancor si crede.

BUTTERFLY
(*rising from the cushion*)

I don't think it, for I know it . . .	Non mi credo: sono . . . sono.

GORO

But the law says:	Ma la legge . . .

BUTTERFLY
(*interrupting*)

What's that to me?	Io non la so.

GORO
(*continuing*)

. . . that the wife who is deserted Has the right to seek divorce.	. . . per la moglie l'abbandono al divorzio equiparò.

BUTTERFLY

That may be Japanese law . . . But not in my country.	La legge giapponese . . . non già del mio paese.

GORO

Which one?	Quale?

BUTTERFLY

The United States.	Gli Stati Uniti.

SHARPLESS

(Poor little creature!)	(Oh, l'infelice!)

BUTTERFLY
(*very nervous, getting more and more excited*)

I know, of course, to open the door And to turn out your wife at any moment, Here, is called divorce. But in America that is not allowed.	Si sa che aprir la porta e la moglie cacciar per la più corta qui divorziar si dice. Ma in America questo non si può.

(*to Sharpless*)

Consul?	Vero?

SHARPLESS
(*embarrassed*)

Why, yes . . . and yet . . . — Vero . . . Però . . .

BUTTERFLY
(*She interrupts him, turning to Yamadori and Goro in triumph.*)

There a good magistrate,
Solemn and wise,
Says to the husband:
'You wish to free yourself?
Let us hear why.'
'I'm sick and tired of
conjugal fetters!'
Then the good judge says:

Là un bravo giudice
serio, impettito,
dice al marito:
'Lei vuole andarsene?
Sentiam perchè?'
'Sono seccato
del coniugato!'
E il magistrato:

(*comically*)

'Ah, wicked scoundrel,
send him to prison!'

'Ah, mascalzone,
presto in prigione!'

(*To put an end to the subject she orders Suzuki:*)

Suzuki, tea. — Suzuki, il thè.

[23]

YAMADORI
(*whispering to Sharpless*)

You hear her? — L'udite?

SHARPLESS

I'm afraid that she will never
Understand.

Mi rattrista una si piena
cecità.

GORO
(*whispering to Sharpless and Yamadori*)

Pinkerton's ship is already
Signalled.

Segnalata è già la nave
di Pinkerton.

YAMADORI
(*in despair*)

And when they meet again . . . — Quand'essa lo riveda . . .

SHARPLESS
(*whispers to both*)

He does not want to see her. That is precisely why
I came to prepare her . . .

Egli non vuol mostrarsi. Io venni appunto
per levarla d'inganno.

(*Seeing that Butterfly, followed by Suzuki, is approaching him to offer him tea, Sharpless cuts short his sentence.*)

BUTTERFLY
(*offering Sharpless tea*)

Will Your Honour allow me . . . — Vostra Grazia permette . . .

(*She opens her fan and, behind it, points to the other two, laughing.*)

What troublesome people. — Che persone moleste!

(*She offers tea to Yamadori who refuses and rises to go.*)

YAMADORI
(*sighing*)

Farewell, then. With heavy heart sighing I leave you
But still I hope . . .

[21] Addio. Vi lascio il cuor pien di cordoglio:
ma spero ancor.

BUTTERFLY

So be it. — Padrone.

YAMADORI
(*He is going out but returns into the room, near Butterfly.*)

If you would only . . . — Ah! se voleste . . .

BUTTERFLY

The pity is: I will not . . . — Il guaio è che non voglio . . .

(*Yamadori, after having bowed to Sharpless, leaves sighing, and gets into a litter.* [22] *The two servants follow him. Butterfly laughs again behind her fan and signs to Suzuki to remove the tea. Suzuki obeys, then retires to the back of the room. Goro eagerly follows Yamadori.*)

[4]

SHARPLESS

(*He assumes a grave and serious look; with great respect, however, and some emotion, he invites Butterfly to be seated and once more draws the letter from his pocket.*)

Well, at last! Now if you please,	Ora a noi. Qui sedete.
Come and sit with me and let me	Legger con me volete
Read this letter.	questa lettera?

(*showing her the letter*)

BUTTERFLY

Show me.	Date.

(*She takes the letter, kisses it and places it on her heart.*)

On my lips, on my heart . . .	Sulla bocca, sul cuore . . .

(*She gives the letter back to Sharpless and says prettily:*)

You're the best man that ever	Siete l'uomo migliore
Existed! Begin, I beg you.	[24] del mondo. Incominciate.

SHARPLESS
(*reading*)

'Dear Friend, I write to ask	'Amico cercherai
You to find my Butterfly.'	quel bel fior di fanciulla . . .'

BUTTERFLY
(*unable to contain herself and interrupting him joyfully*)

Does he really say that?	Dice proprio cosi?

SHARPLESS
(*seriously*)

Yes, he really says it.	Si, cosi dice,
But if you interrupt me . . .	ma se ad ogni momento . . .

BUTTERFLY
(*calming down again to listen*)

I'll be quiet and listen.	Taccio, taccio — più nulla.

SHARPLESS

'Since those happy days together	'Da quel tempo felice
Three years have passed between us.'	tre anni son passati.'

BUTTERFLY
(*interrupting the reading*)

Then he, too, has counted!	Anche lui li ha contati.

SHARPLESS
(*resumes*)

'And maybe Butterfly	'E forse Butterfly
Remembers me no more.'	non mi rammenta più.'

BUTTERFLY
(*surprised, turning to Suzuki*)

I not remember?	Non lo rammento?
Suzuki, tell him quickly.	Suzuki, dillo tu.

(*She repeats, as though scandalised, the words of the letter.*)

'Remembers him no more!'	'Non mi rammenta più!'

(*Suzuki goes out with the tea through the door on the left.*)

SHARPLESS
(to himself)

(Have patience!) (Pazienza!)

(continuing to read)

'If she cares for me 'Se mi vuole
Still and expects me . . .' bene ancora, se mi aspetta . . .'

BUTTERFLY
(She takes the letter from him and exclaims very tenderly:)

Oh, what wonderful tidings! Oh le dolci parole!

(kissing the letter)

You blessed letter! Tu benedetta!

SHARPLESS
(He takes the letter back and boldly resumes reading though his voice is trembling with emotion.)

'I place myself in your hands 'A voi mi raccomando
But act discreetly, and with all due caution perchè vogliate con circospezione
Please prepare her . . .' prepararla . . .'

BUTTERFLY
(anxious, but joyful)

He's coming . . . Ritorna . . .

SHARPLESS

'for the blow which . . .' 'al colpo . . .'

BUTTERFLY
(rises, jumping for joy and clapping her hands)

Tell me. Quando?
Quickly! Quickly! Presto! Presto!

SHARPLESS
(Taking a deep breath, he puts the letter away again; to himself:)

(How can I? (Benone.
How on earth can I tell her? Qui troncarla conviene . . .

(angrily)

That devil of a Pinkerton!) Quel diavolo d'un Pinkerton!)

(He rises, then looks straight into Butterfly's eyes, very gravely.)

Now tell me, Ebbene,
Madam Butterfly, what would you do che fareste Madama Butterfly
If I should tell you he'll return no more? s'ei non dovesse ritornar più mai?

BUTTERFLY
(Motionless, as though she had received a death-blow, she bows her head and replies with childlike submissiveness, almost stammering.)

Two things I might do: Due cose potrei fare:
Go back . . . and entertain tornare a divertire
The people with my songs . . . la gente col cantare
Or else, better, to die. oppur, meglio, morire.

SHARPLESS
(Sharpless is deeply moved and walks up and down excitedly; then he turns to Butterfly, takes her hands in his and says to her with fatherly tenderness:)

Though I feel for you and hate Di strapparvi assai mi costa
To see you suffer these illusions, dai miraggi ingannatori.
I must urge you to accept Accogliete la proposta
The hand of wealthy Yamadori. di quel ricco Yamadori.

BUTTERFLY
(withdrawing her hands)

You, good sir, you tell me this? . . . Voi, signor, mi dite questo!

SHARPLESS
(embarrassed)

Holy Powers, what can I do? Santo Iddio, come si fa?

BUTTERFLY

(*She claps her hands and Suzuki hastens in.*)

Here, Suzuki, please come quickly. Show His Honour to the door.	Qui, Suzuki, presto, presto, che Sua Grazia se ne va.

SHARPLESS

You dismiss me?	Mi scacciate?

(*Butterfly, repenting, runs to Sharpless sobbing and holds him back.*)

BUTTERFLY

I beseech you, Let my words be quite forgotten.	Ve ne prego, già l'insistere non vale.

(*She dismisses Suzuki who goes into the garden.*)

SHARPLESS

(*making excuses*)

I was brutal, I admit it.	Fui brutale, non lo nego.

BUTTERFLY

(*mournfully, laying her hand on her heart*)

Oh, you've wounded me so deeply, Wounded me so very deeply!	Oh, mi fate tanto male, tanto male, tanto, tanto!

(*Butterfly totters, Sharpless is about to support her, but she rallies quickly.*)

Nothing, thank you!	Niente, niente!
I felt ready to die . . . but see, it passes, Swift as shadows that flit across the ocean. Ah, I had forgotten.	Ho creduto morir. Ma passa presto come passan le nuvole sul mare . . . Ah! . . . mi ha scordata?

(*She runs into the room on the left and returns triumphantly carrying her baby on her left shoulder. She shows him to Sharpless, full of pride.*) [25]

Look here, then! See here then! Look here, then! Can such as he well be forgotten?	E questo? e questo? e questo egli potrà pure scordare? . . .

(*She puts the child down on the ground but keeps him close to her.*)

SHARPLESS

(*deeply touched*)

Is it his?	Egli è suo?

BUTTERFLY

(*pointing to each feature*)

No Japanese Boy was ever born with eyes as blue as these are. Such lips too? And such a head of Golden ringlets?	Chi vide mai a bimbo del Giappone occhi azzurini? E il labbro? E i ricciolini d'oro schietto?

SHARPLESS

(*more and more moved*)

He's so like him. Has Pinkerton been told?	È palese. E . . . Pinkerton lo sa?

BUTTERFLY

(*passionately*)

No. I bore him when he had Left me to go back to his country.	No. È nato quando già egli stava in quel suo grande paese.

(*caressing the child*)

But you will write and tell him there awaits him A son who has no equal! And would you tell me, then, that he won't hasten Over land, over sea?	Ma voi gli scriverete che lo aspetta un figlio senza pari! e mi saprete dir s'ei non s'affretta per le terre e pei mari!

(*She puts the baby down on the cushion, kissing him tenderly.*)

Do you know, my darling,	Sai tu cos'ebbe cuore

(pointing to Sharpless)

What that gentleman suggested?
That your mother should take
You on her shoulder, and even wander in rain and
Tempest through the town,
seeking to earn enough for food and clothing,
And then, before the pitying people
To dance in measure to her song, and cry out:
'Listen for the love of all
The eight hundred thousand gods and goddesses of Japan!'
And there will pass a band of valiant warriors
With their Emperor, to whom I'll say:
'Noble Ruler, tarry thy footsteps
And deign to stop and look

di pensar quel signore?
[26] Che tua madre dovrà
prenderti in braccio ed alla pioggia e al vento
andar per la città
a guadagnarti il pane e il vestimento.
*9 Ed alle impietosite
genti, ballando de' suoi canti al suon,
gridare: 'Udite, udite,
udite la bellissima canzon
delle ottocentomila
divinità vestite di splendor.'
[27] E passerà una fila
di guerrieri coll'Imperator,
cui dirò: — 'Sommo duce
ferma i tuoi servi e sosta a riguardar

(holding up the child and fondling it)

At these blue eyes, as blue as the azure heaven
Whence you, Most High are come!'

quest'occhi, ove la luce
dal cielo azzurro onde scendesti appar.'

(She crouches down beside the child and continues in caressing and tearful tones.)

And then, the noble King
Will stay his progress, full of gracious kindness,

[26] E allor fermato il piè
l'Imperatore d'ogni grazia degno,

(laying her cheek against the baby's cheek)

Who knows? He'll make of you
The most exalted ruler of his kingdom.

forse farà di te
[27] il principe più bello del suo regno.

(She presses the child to her heart then, crouching down on the ground, hugs him passionately.)

SHARPLESS

(unable to restrain his tears)

(Poor little thing!)

(Quanta pietà!)

(conquering his emotion)

'Tis evening. I must be going.

Vien sera. Io scendo al piano.

(Butterfly rises to her feet and, with a charming gesture, gives Sharpless her hand; he shakes it cordially with both of his.)

Will you forgive me?

Mi perdonate?

---

*9 The 1906 text includes this uncharacteristically self-pitying song. The music remained the same.

BUTTERFLY

And dance before the kindly
People, as once before so long ago,
And cry out: 'Oh, listen, good people,
Oh listen to my song,
I beg you pity
A helpless mother and her starving son.'

Ed alle impietosite
genti, la man tremante stenderà!
gridando: Udite, udite,
la triste mia canzone.
A un'infelice madre
la carità, muovetevi a pietà!

(She gets up, while the baby stays sitting on the cushion, playing with a doll.)

Oh can it be that Butterfly
Once more shall have to dance for you?
As once in days gone by
Must the Geisha sing again?

E Butterfly, orribile
destino, danzerà per te!
E come fece già
la Ghesha canterà!

(She begs him, with hands raised.)

The joyous song of my youth
Would be broken with a sob and with a sigh!

E la canzon giuliva
e lieta in un singhiozzo finirà!

(throwing herself to her knees in front of Sharpless)

But no, no, not again,
That cursed doorway I shall never enter!
Ah no, never! I'd rather die!
For death were better far than such dishonour!

No! no! questo mai!
questo mestier che al disonore porta!
Morta! Mai più danzar!
Piuttosto la mia vita vo' troncar!
Ah! morta!

(She falls to the ground by the child, whom she holds tightly to her, caressing him convulsively.)

BUTTERFLY
(to the child)

Now you give him your hand, love. | A te, dagli la mano.

SHARPLESS
(He takes the child in his arms.)

What pretty golden ringlets! | I bei capelli biondi!
(kissing him)
Tell me, what do they call you? | Caro: come ti chiamano?

BUTTERFLY

Give answer: | Rispondi:
Sir, my name now is Sorrow. But yet | Oggi il nome è: Dolore. Però
Write and say to my father: on the day | dite al babbo, scrivendogli, che il giorno
Of his return [19] del suo ritorno
Joy shall be my name. | Gioia, mi chiamerò.

SHARPLESS

Your father shall be told, I promise. | Tuo padre lo saprà, te lo prometto.

(He puts down the child, bows to Butterfly and goes out quickly by door on the right.)

SUZUKI
(from outside, shouting)

Scoundrel! Rascal! Wretched viper! | Vespa! Rospo maledetto!

(Suzuki enters, dragging in Goro roughly, who tries in vain to escape. He cries out loudly.)

BUTTERFLY

Who's that? | Che fu?

SUZUKI

He crawls around here, [15] Ci ronza intorno
Evil reptile; from morn to evening | il vampiro! e ogni giorno
And tells the scandal | ai quattro venti
All through the town | spargendo va
That no-one knows | che niuno sa
Who is the baby's father. | chi padre al bimbo sia!

(She releases Goro.)

GORO
(protesting in frightened tones)

I only told her [15] Dicevo solo
That out in America | che là in America
(approaching the child and pointing to him)
That when a baby | quando un figliolo
Is born in such conditions, | è nato maledetto,
(Butterfly instinctively stands in front of the child as though to protect him.)
Then he'll be shunned throughout his life | trarrà sempre reietto
And treated as an outcast! | la vita fra le genti!

(Butterfly, with a wild cry, runs to the shrine and takes down the dagger which hangs there.)

BUTTERFLY

Ah! you're lying, lying! | Ah! menti! menti!
(Butterfly seizes Goro, who falls down; she threatens to kill him. Goro utters loud, desperate and prolonged howls.)
Say it again and I'll kill you! | Dillo ancora e t'uccido!

SUZUKI
(thrusting herself between them)

No! | No!

(Horrified at such a scene, she takes the baby and carries him into the room on the left.)

BUTTERFLY
(Seized with disgust, she pushes Goro away with her foot.)

Get out! | Va via!

(*Goro makes his escape. Butterfly remains motionless as though petrified. By degrees she rouses herself and goes to put away the dagger, her thoughts flying to her child.*)

You'll see, love of my heart, [25]	Vedrai, piccolo amore,
My grief and yet my comfort,	mia pena e mio conforto,
That your avenger soon,	che il tuo vendicator
Soon will be here, to take you and me to his own country, take you and me afar.	ci porterà lontan nella sua terra, lontan ci porterà.

(*A cannon-shot.*)

SUZUKI

(*coming in breathlessly*)

The harbour cannon!	Il cannon del porto!

(*They run towards the terrace.*) [19]

Look, it's a man-of-war!	Una nave da guerra.

BUTTERFLY

(*breathless with excitement*)

White . . . white . . . the American	Bianca . . . bianca . . . il vessillo americano
Stars and stripes! It's putting	delle stelle . . . Or governa
Into port to anchor!	per ancorare.

(*She takes a telescope from the table and runs on to the terrace to look out. Trembling with excitement, she directs the telescope towards the harbour and says to Suzuki:*)

Keep my hand steady	Reggimi la mano
So I can read	ch'io ne discerna
The name, the name. Where is it? Here it is: ABRAHAM	il nome, il nome, il nome. Eccolo: ABRAMO
LINCOLN!	LINCOLN!

(*She gives the telescope to Suzuki and comes down from the terrace in the greatest state of excitement.*)

They all were liars!	Tutti han mentito!
Liars! Liars! But I	tutti! . . . tutti! . . . sol io
Knew it always, yes, I who love him!	lo sapevo . . . io, che l'amo.

(*to Suzuki*)

Now do you see the folly	Vedi lo scimunito
Of doubting? He's coming! He's coming!	tuo dubbio? È giunto! è giunto!
Just at the moment	proprio nel punto
You were all saying: Weep and forget him.	che mi diceva ognun: piangi e dispera.

(*She takes a little American flag from among various toys on the table and gives it to the child.*)

[Now my baby *10	Or bimbo mio
wave your flag high:	alto fa sventolar la tua bandiera:
Now I will call you Joy.]	*Gioia*, or ti chiami.

(*She picks him up and carries him out to the terrace under the branches of a cherry tree in bloom; to Suzuki:*)

Shake that cherry tree till every flower [28]	Scuoti quella fronda
White as snow, flutters down.	di ciliegio e lo innonda di fior.

(*to the child*)

[Clap your hands — your dear, dear hands . . .]	Batti le mani — Care, care le tue mani . . .

*10 This speech was shortened after the first performance for the 1904 Brescia production.

BUTTERFLY

My love wins the day!	Trionfa il mio
See my love and my faith have won completely.	amor, trionfa la mia fede intera.
He's here, he loves me!	Ei torna e m'ama.

(*Rejoicing, she runs on to the terrace. Then, to Suzuki, who has followed her:*)

Shake that cherry tree [28]	Scuoti quella fronda
Till every flower, white as snow,	di ciliegio e m'innonda il fior.
Flutters down; his noble brow in sweet-scented shower	Io vo' tuffare nella pioggia odorosa
I would smother.	l'arsa fronte.

(*sobbing with happiness*)

SUZUKI

(*soothing her*)

Ah, Cho-Cho-San,	Signora
Be calm, I pray, this weeping . . .	quetatevi: quel pianto . . .

BUTTERFLY

No. Laughing, laughing! When may	No! rido, rido! Quanto
We expect him up here?	lo dovremo aspettare?
What do you think? In an hour?	Che pensi? Un'ora?

SUZUKI

Too soon.	Di più.

BUTTERFLY

(*thoughtfully*)

[Certainly more.]	Certo di più.
Two hours more likely.	Due ore forse. Tu

(*walking up and down the room*)

Flowers, flowers, yes, everywhere	va per fiori. Che qui tutto sia pieno
As close as stars are in the heavens.	di fior, come la notte è di faville.

(*She motions to Suzuki to go into the garden.*)

Pick the flowers as if the wind had blown them.	Sfronda tutto il giardin come fa il vento.
And quickly set thousands of lanterns flaming.	E accenderem mille lanterne almeno.
We surely have a thousand . . .	E forse più di mille . . .
No?	No?
We're not so rich?	Siam povere?
A hundred . . . Fifty . . .	Cento . . . Dieci . . .
Whatever the number,	Il conto qual sia
The flame shall glow like the flame in my soul.	la maggior fiamma è nell'anima mia.

[29]

SUZUKI

(*from the terrace*)

Every flower? . . .	Tutti i fior? . . .

BUTTERFLY

(*gaily to Suzuki*)

Every flower. Peaches, violets, jessamine,	Tutti. Pesco, viola, gelsomin,
Every branch of cherry blossom, every flowering tree. [29]	quanto di cespo, o d'erba, o d'albero fiori.

SUZUKI

Desolate as in winter the garden will appear.	Uno squallor d'inverno sarà tutto il giardino.

BUTTERFLY

Ah, but the balmy breath of spring shall breathe her sweetness here. [30]	Tutta la primavera voglio che olezzi qui.

SUZUKI

(*She appears on the terrace with a bunch of flowers which she holds out to Butterfly.*)

Here's more, dear mistress.	A voi, signora.

BUTTERFLY

(*taking the flowers*)

It's not enough yet.	Cogline ancora.

(*Butterfly distributes the flowers about the room, while Suzuki goes down into the garden again.*)

SUZUKI

(*from the garden*)

How often at this window you've stood and wept and waited,	Soventi a questa siepe veniste a riguardare
Gazing and gazing at the deserted world beyond.	lungi, piangendo nella deserta immensità.

BUTTERFLY

No more need I pray, since the kind sea has brought him.	Giunse l'atteso, nulla ormai più chiedo al mare;
Tears to the earth I have given and it returns me flowers!	[31] diedi pianto alla zolla, essa i suoi fior mi dà.

SUZUKI

(*She reappears on the terrace, laden with flowers.*)

Not a flower left.	Spoglio è l'orto.

BUTTERFLY

(*taking the flowers*)

Not a flower left?	Qua il tuo carco.
Come and help me.	Vien, m'aiuta.

(*They scatter flowers everywhere.*)

SUZUKI

Roses shall adorn	Rose al varco
The threshold.	della soglia.

BUTTERFLY AND SUZUKI

Balmy breath of spring shall	[31] Tutta la primavera
Breathe her sweetness here.	voglio che olezzi qui
Let us sow fair April here.	Seminiamo intorno april.

SUZUKI

Lilies ? Violets?	Gigli? viole?

BUTTERFLY

Come scatter flowers all over.	. . . intorno spandi.
Now round his chair	Il suo sedil
Make a garland,	di convolvi s'inghirlandi,
This convolvulus entwining.	di convolvi s'inghirlandi.

BUTTERFLY AND SUZUKI

Lilies and roses let us scatter,	Gigli e viole intorno spandi,
Let us sow fair April here.	Seminiamo intorno april.

(*scattering flowers while they sway their bodies lightly to and fro to the rhythm in a dance measure*)

In handfuls let us scatter	[32] Gettiamo a mani piene
Violets and mimosa	mammole e tuberose,
And sprays of sweetest roses,	corolle di verbene,
Petals of every flower!	petali d'ogni fior!

(*Suzuki places two lamps near the dressing-table over which Butterfly is bending.*)

BUTTERFLY

(*to Suzuki*)

Suzuki, come and help.	Vienni ad ornar . . .

*11

(*Suzuki goes into the room on the left and brings out the baby whom she seats next to Butterfly, while the latter looks at herself in a small hand-mirror and says sadly*:)

How changed he'll find me! . . .	Ahimè, non son più quella!
Drawn weary mouth from far too much sighing,	Troppi sospiri la bocca mandò,
And poor tired eyes	e l'occhio riguardò
From overmuch crying!	nel lontan troppo fiso.

(*She throws herself on the ground, laying her head on Suzuki's feet; ardently*)

Suzuki, make me pretty, make me pretty!	Suzuki, fammi bella, fammi bella!

(*She raises her head and looks into Suzuki's face, crying bitterly.*)

---

*11 In the 1906 version, Suzuki fetches the child at this point, and the stage direction indicates that the sun begins to set. There is an extra line:

No, first bring me the child!	No. Pria, portami il bimbo.

SUZUKI
(*stroking Butterfly's head to soothe her*)

Rest calm and happy, and you'll be fair once more.	Gioia e riposo accrescono beltà.

BUTTERFLY
(*pensively*)

Who knows! Who knows!	Chissà! Chissà!

(*Rising, she goes back to her toilet. To Suzuki*:)

Put on each cheek A little touch of carmine . . .	Dammi sul viso un tocco di carmino . . .

(*She takes a paint-brush and puts a dab of rouge on the baby's cheek.*)

And also for my darling, So that the watching may not make his face Heavy and pallid with shadows.	ed anche a te piccino perchè la veglia non ti faccia vote per pallore le gote.

SUZUKI
(*urging Butterfly to keep quiet*)

Yes, but keep still, till I've finished arranging your hair.	*[12] Non vi movete che v'ho a ravviare i capelli.

BUTTERFLY
(*obeying*) [15]

What a surprise For all my relations! And for the Bonze My uncle! How they Will prate and shout in chorus! Oh what a hubbub The gossips make with Goro! All of them truly Glad of my downfall! And Yamadori With his airs and graces! My scorn And derision, My jeers and contempt For the wretches!	Che ne diranno ora i parenti! E che dira lo zio Bonzo? Qual cicalio faronna in coro le comari con Goro. Già del mio danno tutti contenti! [21] E Yamadori coi suoi languori! Beffati, scornati, spennati gl'ingrati!

*[12] This text was substituted for the 1904 Brescia production.

BUTTERFLY
(*following up an idea she has had*) [15]

This will surprise them! And the Bonze!	Che ne diranno E lo zio Bonzo?

(*with a touch of fury*)

All of them truly Glad of my downfall!	Già del mio danno tutti contenti!

(*smiling*)

And Yamadori With his airs and graces! My scorn And derision, My jeers and contempt For the wretches!	[21] E Yamadori coi suoi languori! Beffati, scornati, spennati gl'ingrati!

SUZUKI
(*She has finished Butterfly's toilet.*)

I've finished.	È fatto.

BUTTERFLY

Bring me now my wedding garment.	L'obi che vestii da sposa.

(*Suzuki goes to a small chest and brings out two garments; one is the white dress with the obi, which she gives to Butterfly.*) [16]

SUZUKI

(*She has finished Butterfly's toilet.*)

I've finished.	E fatto.

BUTTERFLY

Bring me now my wedding garment.	L'obi che vestii da sposa.

(*Suzuki goes to a small chest and looks for the white robe and the obi, while Butterfly pulls the child towards her.*)

[Dear thoughtful little face!]	Cara faccia pensosa!

(*She gets down on her knees and sings a lullaby.*)

[It is Rosy, a little blonde baby like the sun after the storm: the deep blue eyes . . .]	E Roje un bimbo biondo simil a sole dopo la tempesta: l'azzurro occhio profondo . . .

SUZUKI

(*She comes back with two robes and gives one with the obi to Butterfly.*)

Here is the wedding garment.	Ecco l'obi nuzial.

BUTTERFLY

(*She puts down the child.*)

Bring it to me quickly.	Qua ch'io lo vesta.

(*While Butterfly dons her garment, Suzuki dresses the baby in the other one, wrapping him up almost entirely in the light and ample draperies.*)

I would have him see me just As on my wedding day. In my hair we will put a Scarlet poppy . . .	Vo' che mi veda indosso il vel del primo dì. E un papavero rosso nei capelli . . .

(*Suzuki places the flower in Butterfly's hair. The latter is pleased with the effect.*)

Like this.	Così.

(*With child-like grace she signs to Suzuki to close the* shosi. *Night falls.*)

In the *shosi* we'll make three little holes So we can look out, And still as little mice we will stay here To watch and wait. [15, 8b]	Nello *shosi* or farem tre forellini per riguardar, e starem zitti come topolini ad aspettar.

The night grows darker. Suzuki closes the shosi *at the back. Butterfly leads the baby to the* shosi. *She makes three holes in the* shosi*: one high up for herself, one lower down for Suzuki and a third lower still for the child whom she seats on a cushion, signing to him to look through his hole. Suzuki, having brought over the two lamps near the* shosi, *crouches down and also gazes out. Butterfly stands in front of the highest hole and gazes through it, remaining rigid and motionless as a statue: the baby, who is between his mother and Suzuki, peeps out curiously. It is night and the rays of the moon light up the* shosi *from behind. The baby falls asleep, sinking down on his cushion. Suzuki, still in her crouching position, falls asleep too; Butterfly alone remains rigid and motionless.* [24]

A weary night of watching passes. [8a, 33] *The clanging of chains and anchors and the distant voices of sailors rise from the harbour at the foot of the hill.* [10] *When the curtain rises, it is already dawn* [34]; *Butterfly, still motionless, is gazing out into the distance.* [11] *At length she rouses herself and touches Suzuki on the shoulder. The latter wakes with a start and rises, whilst Butterfly turns towards the baby and takes him up with tender care.**13

BUTTERFLY

(*going up the staircase*)

Sweet are you sleeping, Cradled on my heart; Safe in God's keeping, [25]	Dormi amor mio, dormi sul mio cor. Tu sei con Dio

---

*13 The second act was divided into separate acts for the Brescia production in 1904. At that time the dawn sequence was also altered:

SUZUKI

(*awaking with a start*)

It's morning . . .	Già il sole . . .

(*She goes towards Butterfly and touches her gently on the shoulder.*)

Cho-Cho-San!	Cio-Cio-San!

While I must weep apart.
Around your head
The moonbeams dart:
Sleep, my beloved!

ed io col mio dolor.
A te i rai
degli astri d'or:
dormi tesor!

SUZUKI
(*watching her go upstairs and saying with great pity:*)

Poor Madam Butterfly!

Povera Butterfly!

BUTTERFLY
(*stopping, to Suzuki:*)

He'll come — he'll come — you'll see.

Verrà — verrà — vedrai.

(*She enters the room above. Suzuki puts down the lamps which she has extinguished and kneels before the image of the Buddha, as Butterfly's voice becomes quieter and quieter. Then she rises and goes to open the* shosi. [35] *There is a soft knocking at the door.*)

SUZUKI

Who is it? . . .

Chi sia? . . .

(*More knocking. She goes to open the door and cries out in great surprise:*)

Oh! . . .

Oh! . . .

PINKERTON
(*motioning Suzuki to be silent*)

Quiet! Quiet!

Zitta! zitta!

SHARPLESS
(*on the threshold, also motioning her to be silent*)

Sh! . . . Quiet . . . quiet.

Stz! . . . Zitta! zitta!

(*Pinkerton and Sharpless enter cautiously on tiptoe.*)

PINKERTON
(*anxiously to Suzuki*)

Don't let her hear!

Non la destare.

SUZUKI

She was so very weary! She stood and watched for you
All through the night with the baby.

Era stanca si tanto! Vi stette ad aspettare
tutta la notte col bimbo.

Footnote [13] continued. (Brescia, 1904)

BUTTERFLY
(*She starts and says confidently:*)

He'll come. I know he'll come.

Verrà col pieno sole.

(*Butterfly sees the child has fallen asleep and takes him in her arms, turning to go up to the room above.*)

SUZUKI

I beg you, go and rest, for you are weary,
And I will call you when he arrives.

Salite a riposare, affranta siete.
Al suo venire tosto vi chiamerò

BUTTERFLY
(*going up the staircase*)

Sweet are you sleeping,
Cradled on my heart;
Safe in God's keeping,
While I must weep apart.
Around your head
The moonbeams dart:
Sleep, my beloved!

Dormi amor mio,
dormi sul mio cor.
Tu sei con Dio
ed io col mio dolor.
A te i rai
degli astri d'or:
bimbo mio, dormi!

(*She enters the room above.*)

SUZUKI

Poor little Butterfly!

Povera Butterfly!

PINKERTON

How did she know? | Come sapea? . . .

SUZUKI

For three years
Now no ship has put into this port whose flags and colours
Butterfly has not eagerly seen and examined.

Non giunge
da tre anni una nave nel porto, che da lunge
Butterfly non ne scruti il color, la bandiera.

SHARPLESS
(to Pinkerton)

What did I tell you? . . . | Ve lo dissi?! . . .

SUZUKI
(going)

I'll call her . . . | La chiamo . . .

PINKERTON
(stopping her)

No, not yet . . . | No, non ancora . . .

SUZUKI
(pointing to the masses of flowers all about the room) [29, 30]

Look around you. Last night
She insisted that all should be covered with flowers.

Lo vedete, ier sera,
la stanza volle sparger di fiori.

SHARPLESS
(touched)

What did I tell you? . . . | Ve lo dissi? . . .

PINKERTON
(troubled)

Oh God! | Che pena!

SUZUKI
(She hears a noise in the garden and goes to look outside the shosi. *She exclaims in surprise.)*

Who's that outside there
In the garden?
A lady!! . . .

Chi c'è là fuori
nel giardino?
Una donna!! . . .

PINKERTON
(He goes to Suzuki and leads her back again, urging her to speak in a whisper.)

Hush! | Zitta !

SUZUKI
(excitedly)

Who is it? Who is it? | Chi è? chi è?

SHARPLESS
(to Pinkerton)

Get it over and tell her. | Meglio dirle ogni cosa.

SUZUKI
(in consternation)

Who is it? Who is it? | Chi è? chi è?

PINKERTON
(embarrassed)

She came with me. | È venuta con me.

SUZUKI

Who is it? Who is it? | Chi è? chi è?

SHARPLESS
(with restraint but deliberately)

She's his wife! | È sua moglie!

SUZUKI

(*Stunned, she raises her arms to heaven, then falls on her knees with her face to the ground.*)

Hallowed the souls of our fathers! All her world
Is plunged in gloom!

Anime sante degli avi! . . . Alla piccina
è spento il sol!

SHARPLESS

(*He soothes Suzuki and raises her from the ground.*)

We came here so early in the morning.
We hoped you'd be alone here, Suzuki, and that you'd give us
Your help and your guidance in our distress.

Scegliemmo quest'ora mattutina
per ritrovarti sola, Suzuki, e alla gran prova
un aiuto, un sostegno cercar con te.

SUZUKI

(*in despair*)

How can I?

Che giova?

(*Sharpless takes Suzuki aside and tries to persuade her into consenting, whilst Pinkerton, getting more and more agitated, wanders about the room, noting every detail.*)

SHARPLESS

(*to Suzuki*)

[35]

I know for such misfortune
There is no consolation.
But the child's future welfare,
You see, must be protected.
This gentle lady,
Who dares not enter,
Will give the child
A mother's care.

Io so che alle sue pene
non ci sono conforti!
Ma del bimbo conviene
assicurar le sorti!
La pietosa
che entrar non osa
materna cura
del bimbo avrà.

SUZUKI

Ah what sorrow!
Do you ask me to go
And tell a mother . . .

Oh me trista!
E volete ch'io chieda
a una madre . . .

SHARPLESS

(*persisting*)

Go now
And speak with that gentle lady
And bring her here . . . and then if
Butterfly should see her, no matter.
For with her own eyes
She will learn the cruel truth of all we dare not tell her.

Suvvia,
parla con quella pia
e conducila qui — s'anche la veda
Butterfly, non importa.
Anzi — meglio se accorta
del vero si facesse alla sua vista.

(*Sharpless pushes her into the garden, where she joins Mrs Pinkerton.*)

PINKERTON *[14]

Oh! The bitter fragrance
Of these flowers.
And nothing is changed here,

Oh! l'amara fragranza
di questi fiori.
Immutata è la stanza

*[14] This sequence was one of the first alterations to the original score, and was made before the second performance (Brescia, 1904) in order to give the tenor an aria.

SHARPLESS

Go, Suzuki, go!

Vieni, Suzuki, vieni! . . .

SUZUKI

Hear my sorrow!

Oh me trista!

PINKERTON

Oh! The bitter fragrance
Of these flowers,

Oh! l'amara fragranza
di questi fiori

Where once we loved . . .	dei nostri amori . . .
(He sees his own portrait and picks it up.)	
And here's my picture!	Il mio ritratto!
(He puts it down.)	
Three years have passed away and every day,	Tre anni son passati — e noverati
Every hour, alas, she counted.	n'ha i giorni e l'ore.
(Agitated by these reminiscences, he turns to Sharpless.)	
I simply cannot stay . . . I'll see you	Non posso rimaner . . . vi aspetto
On the footpath.	per la via.

SHARPLESS

Did I not warn you?	Non ve l'ho detto?

PINKERTON

(taking the Consul's hands in his)

You've seen me weeping girlish tears,	M'avete visto piangere,
And the tears are not easy . . .	nè son facile al pianto . . .
Peace I can never render her,	Pace non posso renderle,
(He gives the Consul some money.)	
But you might bring her some comfort . . .	A voi, qualche soccorso . . .
She must not fall into wretched poverty.	Ch'ella non cada almeno in povertà.
You must speak of the child to her;	Voi del figlio parlatele;
I don't dare to. Oh, how could I?	io non oso. Ho rimorso;

Footnote [14] continued. (Brescia, 1904)

It is poison to my heart.	velenosa al cor mi va.
And nothing is changed here,	Immutata è la stanza
Where once we loved . . .	dei nostri amori . . .
But a deathly chill haunts the air.	ma un gel di morte vi sta.
(He sees his own portrait.)	
And here's my picture!	Il mio ritratto! —
Three years have passed away and every day,	Tre anni son passati — e noverati
Every hour, alas, she counted.	ella n'ha i giorni e l'ore.

(Overcome by emotion and unable to hold back his tears, he comes up to Sharpless and speaks to him resolutely.)

I cannot remain; Sharpless, I'll see you	Non posso rimaner; Sharpless vi
On the footpath.	aspetto per via.

SHARPLESS

Did I not warn you?	Non ve l'avevo detto?

PINKERTON

Give her this money, just to support her . . .	Datele voi qualche soccorso . . .
Remorse and anguish choke me.	Mi struggo dal rimorso.

SHARPLESS

I warned you — you remember?	Vel dissi? vi ricorda?
When in your hand she laid hers:	quando la man vi diede:
'Be careful, for she believes you.'	'Badate! Elle ci crede'
Alas, how true I spoke!	e lui profeta allor!
Deaf to doubting, humiliation,	Sorda ai consigli,
Blindly trusting to your promise,	sorda ai dubbi, vilipesa,
Her heart will break.	nell'ostinata attesa
	raccolse il cor.

PINKERTON

Yes. In one sudden moment	Si, tutto in un istante
I see my heartless action,	io vedo il fallo mio e sento
And feel that I shall never free myself	che di questo tormento
From remorse.	trega mai non avrò! no!

(*as though taking a decision, and putting his hand on his brow*)

I'm so bewildered! Forgive me . . .	sono stordito! addio,
The grief will pass.	mi passerà.

(*He leaves hurriedly while Kate Pinkerton and Suzuki enter from the garden.*)

KATE
(*gently, to Suzuki*)

Then you will tell her?	Glielo dirai?

SUZUKI
(*replying with her head bowed, and still very tense*)

I promise.	Prometto.

KATE

And will you please persuade her She can trust me?	E le darai consiglio di affidarmi? . . .

SUZUKI

I promise.	Prometto.

KATE

As if he were my own son.	Lo terrò come un figlio.

SUZUKI

I trust you but I must be quite alone beside her . . .	Vi credo. Ma bisogna ch'io le sia sola accanto . . .
In this cruel hour alone. She will weep so sadly.	Nella grande ora — sola! Piangerà tanto tanto!

BUTTERFLY
(*calling from the room above*)

Suzuki, where are you?	Suzuki, dove sei?

(*She appears at the head of the staircase.*)

Suzuki! . . .	Suzuki! . . .

SUZUKI
(*signing to the others to keep quiet*)

I'm here . . . I was praying and going back to watch . . .	Son qui . . . pregavo e rimettevo a posto . . .

(*Butterfly begins to come downstairs. Suzuki rushes towards the staircase to prevent her.*)

No . . . Do not come down . . .	No . . . non scendete . . .

BUTTERFLY
(*She comes down quickly, freeing herself from Suzuki who tries in vain to hold her back. Then she paces the room in great but joyful excitement.*)

He's here . . . where is he hidden?	È qui . . . dov'è nascosto?

Footnote [14] continued. (Brescia, 1904)

SHARPLESS

Now go — the cruel truth She best should hear alone. But now this faithful heart Has perhaps already divined.	[7] Andate, il triste vero da sola apprenderà. Ma or quel cor sincero presago è già.

PINKERTON
(*sweetly, with remorse*)

Farewell, O happy home! Farewell, home of love! Haunted for ever shall I be By her reproachful eyes. Farewell, O happy home, I cannot bear to stay, Farewell, farewell, let me fly!	[36] Addio, fiorito asil, di letizia e d'amor. Sempre il mite suo sembiante con strazio atroce vedrò. Addio, fiorito asil, Non reggo al tuo squallor! Fuggo, fuggo, son vil!

(*He shakes the Consul's hands and leaves hurriedly at the back. Sharpless shakes his head sadly. Suzuki enters from the garden, followed by Kate who stops at the foot of the terrace.*)

(*She catches sight of Sharpless.*)

Here's the Consul . . . and where is? . . . where is? . . .	Ecco il Console . . . e . . . dove? dove? . . .

(*She sees Kate in the garden and stares fixedly at Sharpless.*)

Not here!	Non c'è.

(*Having searched everywhere, in every corner, in the little alcove and behind the screen, she is frightened and looks around in alarm..*)

Who are you?	Chi siete?
Why have you come here? . . . No-one answers? . . .	Perchè veniste? . . . Niuno parla! . . .

(*Suzuki weeps silently.*)

Why are you weeping?	Perchè piangete?

(*Sharpless approaches her to speak: she is afraid of understanding and shrinks back like a frightened child.*)

No, no, tell me nothing . . . nothing . . . I might fall	No: non ditemi nulla . . . nulla — forse potrei
Dead at your feet at the words I hear.	cader morta sull'attimo.

(*with affectionate and childlike kindness to Suzuki*)

You, Suzuki, you're always	Tu, Suzuki, che sei
So faithful, don't weep, I pray! Since I know that you love me	tanto buona — non piangere! e mi vuoi tanto bene,
Say 'yes' or 'no' quite softly . . . He lives?	un Si od un No — di' piano . . . Vive?

SUZUKI

Yes.	Si.

BUTTERFLY

(*transfixed as though she had received a mortal blow*)

But he'll come	Ma non viene
No more. They have told you! . . .	più. Te l'han detto! . . .

(*angered at Suzuki's silence*)

Viper! I want you to answer.	Vespa! Voglio che tu risponda.

SUZUKI

No more.	Mai più.

BUTTERFLY

(*coldly*)

He reached here yesterday?	Ma è giunto ieri?

SUZUKI

Yes.	Si.

BUTTERFLY

(*She has understood and looks at Kate as though fascinated.*)

Who is this lady	Quella donna bionda
That makes me so frightened, that makes me so frightened?	mi fa tanta paura! Mi fa tanta paura!

KATE *[15]

(*simply*)

Through no fault of my own, I am the cause of your sorrow.	Son la causa innocente d'ogni vostra sciagura.
Ah, forgive me, pray.	Perdonatemi.

(*She is about to approach Butterfly who imperiously motions her to keep away.*)

BUTTERFLY

No, do not touch me.	No, non mi toccate.

---

*[15] In 1906 Kate's speeches were given to Sharpless.

SHARPLESS

Through no fault of her own, she is	È la causa innocente d'ogni
the cause of your sorrow.	vostra sciagura.
Forgive her, pray.	Perdonatele.

(*There is a long and painful silence; then Butterfly resumes in a calm voice:*)

How long	Quanto
Ago is it since he married you?	tempo è che vi ha sposata — voi?

KATE

A year.	Un anno.
(*shyly*)	
And will you let me do nothing for the child?	[25] E non mi lascerete far nulla pel bambino?
(*Butterfly is silent.*)	
I will tend him with most loving care.	Io lo terrei con cura affettuosa . . .
(*Impressed by Butterfly's silence, and deeply moved, she persists:*)	
'Tis hard for you, very hard,	È triste, triste cosa!
But take this step for his welfare . . .	ma fatelo pel suo meglio . . .

BUTTERFLY

(*She remains motionless.*) [15]

Enough!	Chissà!?
To him I owe my duty.	Tutto è compiuto ormai!

KATE

(*coaxingly*)

Ah, can you not forgive me, Butterfly?	Potete perdonarmi, Butterfly?

BUTTERFLY

(*solemnly*)

Under the vault of the sky there is no	Sotto il gran ponte del cielo non v'è
Happier lady than you are.	donna di voi più felice.
(*passionately*)	
May you remain so,	Siatelo sempre felice
Never be saddened through me.	e non v'attristate per me.
Yet it would please me much that you should tell him	Mi piacerebbe pur che gli diceste
That peace will come to me.	che pace io troverò.

KATE

(*holding out her hand*)

Your hand, your hand, may I not take it?	E la mano . . . la man, me la dareste?

Footnote [15] continued. (Paris, 1906)

BUTTERFLY

(*She has understood and cries out.*)

Ah! It is his wife!	Ah! È sua moglie!
(*in a calm voice*)	
It is all over for me!	Tutto è morto per me!
All is finished! Ah!	Tutto è finito! ah!

SHARPLESS

Have courage.	Coraggio.

BUTTERFLY

They want to take everything from me!	Voglion prendermi tutto!
My son!	Il figlio mio!

SHARPLESS

Make this sacrifice for his welfare . . .	Fatelo pel suo bene il sacrifizio.

BUTTERFLY

(*despairingly*)

Ah! Unhappy mother!	Ah! triste madre!
To abandon my son!	Abbandonar mio figlio!
(*she remains calm and motionless*)	
Enough.	E sia.
To him I owe obedience!	A lui devo obbedir!

BUTTERFLY
(decidedly but kindly)

I pray you, no, not that . . . Now go and leave me.	Vi prego — questo . . . no . . . Andate adesso.

KATE
(going towards Sharpless)

Poor little lady!	Povera piccina!

SHARPLESS
(deeply moved)

Oh, the pity of it all!	È un immensa pietà!

KATE
(whispering to Sharpless)

And can he have his son?	E il figlio lo darà?

BUTTERFLY
(who has heard, says solemnly)

His son I will give him If he himself will fetch him. Climb this hill in half an hour from now. [20]	A lui lo potrò dare se lo verrà a cercare. Fra mezz'ora salite la collina.

*16

(Suzuki takes Kate out of the door on the right and then goes up to the room above: Sharpless goes up to Butterfly, giving her Pinkerton's money.)

Footnote [15] continued. (Paris, 1906)

KATE
(She has timidly approached along the terrace, without coming into the room.)

Ah, can you not forgive me, Butterfly?	Potete perdonarmi, Butterfly?

BUTTERFLY
(solemnly)

Under the vault of the sky there is no Happier lady than you are.	Sotto il gran ponte del cielo non v'è donna di voi liù felice.

(passionately)

May you remain so, Never be saddened through me.	Siatelo sempre felice e non v'attristate per me.

KATE
(to Sharpless, who has come towards her.)

Poor little lady!	Povera piccina!

SHARPLESS
(deeply moved)

Oh, the pity of it all!	È un'immensa pietá!

KATE

And can he have his son?	E il figlio lo darà!

BUTTERFLY
(who has heard, says solemnly and enunciating her words distinctly:)

His son I will give him If he himself will fetch him.	A lui lo potrò dare se lo verrà a cercare.

(meaningfully and with great simplicity:)

Climb this hill half an hour from now.	Fra mezz'ora salite la collina.

(Suzuki escorts Kate and Sharpless who go out at the back. Butterfly falls to the ground weeping — Suzuki hastens to support her.)

---

*16 The following scene was cut in 1906 for Paris and the action continued after Sharpless's departure.

SHARPLESS
(*stammering with emotion*)

[My friend gave me . . .
for you . . . I don't know how to explain . . .
He foresaw . . .]

L'amico mio mi diede . . .
per voi . . . non so spiegarmi . . .
Egli provvede . . .

BUTTERFLY
(*interrupting him*)

[Do not weep, sir, I am used
to worse things. — And then, nevertheless,
it brings certainty.
Hoping and dreaming,
these do not, do not bring peace. —
So if you please . . .
give this back . . .]

Non piangete, signore, io sono avvezza
ad ogni peggior cosa. — E poi riposa
pur tanto una certezza.
La speranza ed il sogno,
quelli no, non dan pace. —
Or se vi piace. —
rendete . . .

(*She thrusts the money at Sharpless.*)

SHARPLESS
(*refusing*)

[Oh no.]

Oh no.

BUTTERFLY

[I do not need it.]

Non me ne fa bisogno.

(*Suzuki comes back into the room from the door on the left and stands to one side, watching.*)

SHARPLESS
(*trying to persaude her by scolding her teasingly*)

[How stubborn is this little head!]

Com'è caparbia quella testolina!

BUTTERFLY
(*resolutely giving him back the money*)

[I wish it.]

Lo voglio.

SHARPLESS
(*taking the money*)

[I will obey.]

Obbedirò.

BUTTERFLY

[Goodbye.]

Addio.

SHARPLESS

[We may meet again?]

Si può rivedervi?

BUTTERFLY

[We may:
climb the hill in half an hour.]

Si può:
fra mezz'ora salite la collina.

(*Sharpless leaves. Butterfly stands up with difficulty: Suzuki hastens to support her.*)

SUZUKI
(*placing her hand on Butterfly's heart*)

Your little fluttering heart is beating
Like a terrified bird in a cage.

Come una mosca prigioniera
l'ali batte il piccolo cuor!

[20]

BUTTERFLY
(*Butterfly gradually recovers; seeing that it is broad daylight, she disengages herself from Suzuki and says to her:*)

Too much light shines outside
And too much laughing spring.
Close them.

Troppa luce è di fuor,
e troppa primavera.
Chiudi.

(*Suzuki goes to shut the screens so that the room is almost in total darkness.* [34 *minor*] *She returns to Butterfly.*)

Where is the child?

Il bimbo ove sia?

SUZUKI

Playing ... Shall I fetch him?

Giuoca ... Lo chiamo?

BUTTERFLY

Leave him where he is
And go and play with him.

Lascialo giuocar.
Va. Fagli compagnia.

SUZUKI
(*refusing*)

I'll not leave you alone. No! No!

Non vi voglio lasciar. No! No!

(*She throws herself weeping at Butterfly's feet.*)

BUTTERFLY
(*affectionately stroking Suzuki's head*)

Yesterday did you not clearly advise me:
That rest and sleep would be better for my looks?

Ieri m'hai detto una savia parole:
che il buon riposo accresce la beltà?

SUZUKI

I did.

Vero.

BUTTERFLY

Leave me alone
And your Butterfly now will go and rest.

Lasciami sola
e la tua Butterfly riposerà.

(*Suzuki refuses to leave.*)

How runs the ditty? 'Through closed gates *[17]
Life and love entered with him, then he went
And nought was left to us,
Nothing, nothing but death.'

Sai la canzone? 'Varcò le chiuse porte,
prese il posto di tutto — se ne andò —
e nulla vi lasciò,
nulla, fuor che la morte.'

SUZUKI
(*weeping*)

I'll stay with you.

Resto con voi.

BUTTERFLY
(*resolutely, clapping her hands loudly*)

Go, go, obey my order.

Va ... va. Te lo comando.

(*She makes the weeping Suzuki rise and pushes her through the door on the left. She lights the lamp in front of the Buddha and remains in front of the image, motionless, lost in sorrowful thoughts.* [15] *Suzuki's sobs are still heard; they die away gradually. Butterfly goes to the shrine and lifts the white veil from it. She throws this across the screen, then takes the dagger which, enclosed in a waxen case, is leaning against the wall near the image of Buddha.* [12] *She piously kisses the blade, holding it in both hands by the point and the handle. She softly reads the words inscribed on it.*)

'Death with honour
Is better than life with dishonour.'

'Con onor muore
Chi non può serbar vita con onore.'

(*She points the knife sideways at her throat. The door on the left opens, showing Suzuki's arm pushing the child towards his mother: he runs in with outstretched hands. Butterfly lets the dagger fall, darts towards the child and hugs and kisses him almost to suffocation.*)

You? you? My little darling,
My dearest treasure.
Fairest flower of beauty.

Tu, tu, piccolo Iddio!
Amore, amore mio.
fior di giglio e di rosa.

(*Taking the child's head in her hands she draws it to her.*)

You must never know it:
'Tis for you, my love, 'tis for you
I'm dying, poor Butterfly,
So you can go away
Beyond the ocean,
Never to feel the torment when you are older
That your mother forsook you!
My son, sent down from Heaven, [37]

Non saperlo mai:
per te, per i tuoi puri
occhi, muor Butterfly,
perchè tu possa andare
di là dal mare
senza che ti rimorda ai dì maturi,
il materno abbandono.
O a me, sceso dal trono

---

*[17] Retained for Brescia but cut for Paris in 1906.

From Paradise descended.	dell'alto Paradiso,
Ah, remember, remember how . . .	guarda ben fiso, fiso
How your mother has loved	di tua madre la faccia! . . .
You and let the memory linger,	che ten' resti una traccia,
So farewell! [Look at me well! . . . So that a	guarda ben!
trace, however pale and little, of your	*18 Sia pur pallida e poca.
mother's face remains to you — so that the	Che non tutto consunto
last bloom of my beauty has not been	vada di mia beltà l'ultimo fior.
wholly wasted.]	
Beloved angel!	Amore, addio!
Farewell, my dearest heart!	Addio, piccolo amor!
Go, play, play.	Va. Gioca, gioca.

Butterfly takes the child, seats him on a stool with his face turned to the left, gives him the American flag and a doll and urges him to play with them while she gently bandages his eyes. Then she seizes the dagger and, with her eyes still fixed on the child, goes behind the screen. The knife is heard falling to the ground and the large white veil disappears behind the screen. Butterfly emerges; tottering, she gropes her way towards the child. The large white veil is round her neck; smiling feebly she grasps the child with her hand and drags herself up to him. She has just enough strength left to embrace him, then falls to the ground beside him. At this moment Pinkerton's voice is heard outside calling repeatedly [20]:

"Butterfly! Butterfly!"

then the door on the right opens violently. [27] *Pinkerton and Sharpless rush into the room and up to Butterfly who, with a feeble gesture, points to the child and then dies. Pinkerton falls on his knees whilst Sharpless takes the child and kisses him, sobbing.*

The curtain falls swiftly.

*18 These three lines were cut after the first performance (1904).

Eiddwen Harrhy (Cio-Cio-San) in the final scene of the ENO production in 1983 (photo: Alex von Koettlitz)

Discography / *David Nice*

All versions are in stereo unless otherwise stated. For detailed analysis and comparison the enthusiast is referred to *Opera on Record*, ed. Alan Blyth (Hutchinson, 1979). Recordings listed in order of issue.

Conductor	*De Fabritiis* (mono — r. 1939)	*Karajan*	*Leinsdorf*	*Serafin*	*Santini*	*Leinsdorf*
Company/ Orchestra	**Rome Opera**	**La Scala, Milan**	**Rome Opera**	**Accademia di Santa Cecilia**	**Rome Opera**	**RCA Italiana**
Butterfly	Dal Monte	Callas	Moffo	Tebaldi	de los Angeles	L. Price
Pinkerton	Gigli	Gedda	Valletti	Bergonzi	Björling	Tucker
Sharpless	Basiola	Borriello	Cesari	Sordello	Sereni	Maero
Suzuki	Palombini	Danieli	Elias	Cossotto	Pirazzini	Elias
LP number	(EMI Italiana) 118408-3 (2)	(EMI) EX291265-3 (2)	—	(Decca) 411 634-1DO3 (3)	(CFP) CFPD414446-3 (2)	—
Tape number	(EMI Italiana) 118408-5 (2)	(EMI) EX291265-5 (2)	—	(Decca) 411 634-4DO2 (2)	(CFP) CFPD414446-5 (2)	—
CD number	—	(EMI) CDS747959-8 (2)	(RCA) GD84145 (2)	(Decca) 425 531-2 (2)	(EMI) CDS749575-2 (2)	(RCA) RD86160 (2)

Conductor	*Barbirolli*	*Karajan*	*Maazel*	*Patané*	*Sinopoli*
Company/ Orchestra	**Rome Opera**	**Vienna State Opera, VPO**	**Ambrosian Opera Ch, Philharmonia**	**Hungarian State Opera**	**Ambrosian Opera Ch, Philharmonia**
Butterfly	Scotto	Freni	Scotto	Kincses	Freni
Pinkerton	Bergonzi	Pavarotti	Domingo	Dvorsky	Carreras
Sharpless	Panerai	Kerns	Wixell	Miller	Berganza
Suzuki	Di Stasio	Ludwig	Knight	Takacs	Pons
LP number	(EMI) EX290839-3 (2)	(Decca) SET 584 (3)	–	–	(DG) 423 567-1GH3 (3)
Tape number	(EMI) EX290839-5 (2)	(Decca) K2A1 (3)	–	–	(DG) 423 567-4GH3 (3)
CD number	(EMI) CMS769654-2 (2)	(Decca) 417 577-2DH3 (3)	(CBS) CD35181 (2)	(Hungaraton) HCD 12256/7 (2)	(DG) 423 567-2GH3 (3)

Bibliography

Mosco Carner has written *Puccini: A Critical Biography* (Duckworth, 1974) which combines rare psychological insight with musical scholarship. It is laid out in three parts (*The Man, The Artist, The Work*) to give a masterly and very readable survey of the subject. Other biographies include Edward Greenfield's *Puccini: Keeper of the Seal* (London, 1958), and William Ashbrook's *The Operas of Puccini* (Cassell, 1969).

The more general reader may be interested in the New Grove *Masters of Italian Opera* (Papermac, 1980), which includes an entry by Mosco Carner on Puccini, as well as essays on Rossini, Bellini, Donizetti and Verdi.